A
COUNTRY
HOUSE
CHRISTMAS

To my children

First published in the United Kingdom in 1952 by
Herbert Jenkins Ltd as Treasure on Earth.

This edition published in the United Kingdom in 2016 by
National Trust Books
1 Gower Street
London
WC1E 6HD

An imprint of Pavilion Books Company Limited.

Text © The Estate of Phyllis Sandeman, courtesy of Nicolette Vincent
Foreword © Mrs F. C. H. Fryer, 1995
Cover design © National Trust Books, 2016

The moral rights of the author have been asserted.

ISBN: 9781911358046

A CIP catalogue record for this book is available from the British
Library.

20 19 18 17 16
10 9 8 7 6 5 4 3 2 1

Reproduction by Mission Productions, Hong Kong
Printed and bound by GPS Group, Slovenia

This book can be ordered direct from the publisher at the website:
www.pavilionbooks.com, or try your local bookshop.
Also available at National Trust shops and nationaltrustbooks.co.uk.

A COUNTRY HOUSE CHRISTMAS

Treasure on Earth

Phyllis Elinor Sandeman

National Trust

Dream of childhood far away,
   Hear the old world calling;
Try to paint the golden day
   Now that night is falling—
Lone in echoing play-grounds seek
   For a vanished throng—
Strive in halting words to speak
   Of a finished song.

Foreword

I AM DELIGHTED to have been asked to write a foreword to the new edition of my aunt's charming book, *Treasure on Earth*. It is a fascinating account, beautifully illustrated by herself, of Christmas at Lyme in the first decade of this century, when she was a little girl.

A generation later, in 1925 when I was just ten years old, I, too, spent an unforgettable Christmas at Lyme. Nine of us in the party of sixteen were children so the fun we had was indescribable! That year, as seemed to happen more frequently in those days, there was a white Christmas and I vividly remember the excitement and almost ecstatic delight of sliding on the frozen lake, tobogganing in the park and having snowball fights with my numerous cousins. In the late afternoon, as it became dark, we would return to the house, accompanied always by the boys' fox terrier, Mike, eat a colossal and delicious school-room tea and then play ping-pong in the Long Gallery. Later we would play games such as Charades and Dumb Crambo in the Hall, which was warmed by an enormous fire and embellished by a magnificent Christmas tree. How we laughed and talked and argued! In those days there was no silent watching of a television screen.

My family and I tremendously appreciate the welcome and kindness shown us when we visit Lyme. We are made to feel as if our roots are still firmly there and that we are in no way outsiders. The links with the past are still apparent and this was brought home to me at my husband's funeral in June 1992. I was deeply touched when a lady came up to me at the tea-party, which had been so kindly arranged for us at

Lyme after the service, and told me that she had been at my husband's coming-of-age celebration at the house in 1936.

He loved Lyme profoundly and that is borne out by the fact that, as a young man, he spent many hours taking photographs of the house and processing and enlarging them in his dark room. He was also very proud of the manual skills taught him as a boy by various employees with whom he greatly enjoyed working in the holidays. In this way he acquired a useful knowledge of carpentry, electrical work and plumbing. Although unable latterly, due to ill health, to visit his old home very often he was tremendously pleased to know it is being maintained and loved as it so richly deserves.

I am certain that this book, about a way of life that will never again be experienced, will give pleasure to many people, both old and young. I hope also that it may, in some measure, illustrate the very deeply held affection felt for Lyme by so many members of different generations of the Legh family.

Priscilla Newton, March 1993

Since the foreword was written, Priscilla, Lady Newton has remarried and is now Mrs F C H Fryer.

KEY to the real identies and place names

For VYNE PARK *read* LYME

For VAYNE OR VYNE *read* LEGH OR LYME

For SIR THOMAS VAYNE *read* 2ND LORD NEWTON

Treasure on Earth

1906

IN THE NORTHERN HALF OF ENGLAND, IN A GREAT HILLY park bordering on three counties, stands an Elizabethan mansion, high amongst its hills on a tableland of lawns and terraces, stone-built round a central courtyard with a long, almost unbroken frontage and three rows of windows looking down the valley. Great stone buttresses support it on one side where the ground falls steeply and at their feet lies an Italian garden. Behind the house the ground rises again to the uninhabited moors.

One Christmas Eve, well before the First World War, a fine layer of snow already covered the slopes of the park and the sky was heavy with more to come. Not far from the house, in a wooded hollow beside a mill pool, deer were feeding from bundles of hay. Passing through this wooded valley, rising in serpentine twists and bends, a carriage drive wound its gradual ascent to the house, but cutting across it, running straight up the steep hillside, a narrow footpath gave a direct approach. Up this a little girl was climbing. She wore the black stockings and button-boots of her generation, an obviously home-made coat and skirt, and a hat secured by an elastic under her chin.

It was late afternoon.

Rabbits, looking almost black in the fading light, sped to their snowy burrows on either side of the path. A cock pheasant rocketed up almost from the child's feet and made for the cover of the woods. Without pausing, she continued on her way. Excitement was mounting in her as she climbed. So short a time to wait now before the curtain rose on a drama of infinite delight—a gradual crescendo of bliss. To-night a large party of visitors was arriving, and from to-morrow for a whole fortnight one pleasure would succeed another.

There might, if this weather held, be skating or better still tobogganing, for which the slopes of the park were so well suited—but the weather did not matter. How could it, with a house full of delightful visitors and such a house to play in? There would be the Christmas tree with all its presents; games in the drawing-room, music and dancing in the hall, private theatricals in the Long Gallery; hide-and-seek all over the house, with people chasing each other in delicious terror the whole length of the long corridors; wonderful meals in the dining-room, dinners as well as luncheons even for little girls, and all the time everybody, particularly the grown-ups, happy, good-humoured, joking and jolly, ready at any moment to romp and play the fool.

This heavenly drama was just due to begin, and nothing short of some utterly remote possibility, severe illness or sudden death, could prevent it from happening—but quite rightly such a possibility never entered the child's head.

At the top of the slope, where the footpath emerging from behind a row of old lime trees joined the drive just in front of the forecourt, the house was fully revealed. Lights shone in some of the windows glowing warmly behind red blinds. The Tudor mullions had been replaced by sash windows in the time of Charles II and the only portion of the façade still in its original state was the gate-house in the centre. Two small guard houses with barred windows and surmounted by couching lions flanked the wide-open gates of the forecourt.

The main approach to the house was a continuous ascent, the ground on the right hand falling away to wooded declivities, on the left rising in stretches of open country to a panorama of distant hills. Above the tree-tops in the middle distance rose a bare conical hill, its summit crowned by an ancient grey stone tower.

Suddenly the air was filled with the clamour of an army of rooks. The whole western slope of the hill was black with these birds, which every evening assembled here and, remaining for a few moments silent, as if in prayer, then dispersed to their roosting places in the lime trees near the house.

Still thinking of nothing but the coming delights, the child turned in at the forecourt gates. To her the house seemed to possess a living soul of its own and to be now waiting in a state of happiness that matched her own to take the arriving guests into its loving old heart.

From a mediæval manor standing in a royal forest it

had been enlarged to its present dimensions in the time of Elizabeth, but ever since its origin and the grant of land by Edward the Black Prince to Sir Piers Vayne it had known no other owners but his direct descendants.

Each successive generation had left its impress on the place, adding to, altering and embellishing the original structure in lavish expenditure of material means and tender devotion, till it had become what it now was—a palace, but lived in and loved as a home.

The big central doorway led straight into the cloistered courtyard round which the house was built. Opposite, across the courtyard, another door led out to the terrace and gardens. But the child was bound for the housekeeper's room, which opened off the cloisters, a very pleasant place to visit before going upstairs and where a warm welcome was always assured. Now, bursting in as usual, she found her friend Mrs. Campbell in best black dress and lace cap seated in her chair by the fire. The curtains were drawn and the table laid for tea for at least a dozen people.

Mrs. Campbell exclaimed at her appearance: "Good gracious, Miss Phyllis, you've never been out in all this cold in only that thin jacket! And where are your snow boots?"

"Oh, there's hardly any snow yet; it's all right. I want to find Jim Bowden and ask him to make us something for the play. Have you seen him? He's not down at the workshop—I've just come from there."

Clicking her tongue, the housekeeper wondered for the hundredth time why Lady Vayne, her mistress, did not bother more about the child's clothes. Who would have thought that the parents of this poorly clad little figure were the owners of Vyne Park! But it was an age when the children of the upper classes were not as a rule much cosseted or even very well dressed, a strange whim or fancy obtaining amongst the richest and most privileged set of people in the civilised world. By this time many children of very rich parents without much tradition might be seen disporting themselves in Hyde Park and Hamilton Gardens arrayed like exotic birds in velvets and furs. Amongst them flitted the children of the English aristocracy, clothed, as if simplicity were not enough, often in shabby, outgrown garments, the discards of their elder brothers and sisters. In the adult world, too, extreme comfort mingled with austerity. Many, of whom Sir Thomas Vayne was one, took cold baths throughout the year; even in the rigorous climate of northern England short tweed jackets were worn out of doors in winter, boots lined with lambswool were unknown, fur coats were reserved for carriage wear and fur jackets for children were not approved of, for the cult of the child had not yet set in.

Mrs. Campbell, however, thought differently, and Phyllis had to repeat her question before she received an answer.

"Jim! He'll be messing about on the stage in the Long Gallery I expect. Come and get warm, dear; you look half perished with cold."

"I thought they finished putting up the stage this morning."

"So they did according to Mr. Truelove, but Jim would be there when he's wanted elsewhere. There's a handle off the chest of drawers in the Oak Room where Mr. Blunt's going, and what he'll think I don't know."

"Where's Alethea going to sleep?"

"Why, in one of the tower rooms, of course."

The tower, two-storeyed and cube-shaped, behind the pediment on the Palladian side of the house, had been added in the early nineteenth century by a Vayne with more money than taste who wanted extra room to house the servants of his guests. Mrs. Campbell slept in it, as did the visiting ladies' maids, and occasionally when the house

was very full the children of visitors. There was no water laid on and every drop had to be carried from the floor below up a narrow, twisting staircase. Before the purity of the south front had been marred by this addition there had stood another tower, octagonal in shape, with a pointed roof, which figured in early pictures of the house. This was removed to make room for the new tower and, the craze for follies being at its height, re-erected on the edge of the moors behind the house; and here 'the Lantern,' as it was called, still stood.

People coming to Vyne for the first time were always struck by its two outstanding features: the extraordinary setting—a palace and gardens on the edge of the wilderness—and the strangely harmonious marriage of two widely different styles of architecture, Elizabethan and Palladian.

From the north one entered by the Tudor gatehouse

(experts had pronounced it to be pre-Elizabeth) passed into the Italianate courtyard, with its massive pillars and arches, through a wide and deep arcade and emerged under the pillared portico of the neo-classical south front. To the right the house's western flank verged on a sheer drop of forty feet to where the Italian garden lay beneath the supporting walls. To the left the ground rose in a series of terraces with wide flights of steps. In front beyond the stretch of lawn lay a tree-bordered, islanded lake fed by a rushing, tumbling little hill-stream; beyond this a lime avenue leading upwards to a wood of larch and fir; beyond this the moors.

It was the embodiment of a poet's dreams—Arcadian idylls, faery lands forlorn; and once seen was not easy to forget. With his genius for spending money both un-profitably and disastrously, the builder of the tower had conceived the idea of draining the moors, with the result that, never again clothed in the purple of heather, they remained dun-coloured throughout the year, and the once-plentiful grouse also departed. Even so, he had been unable to destroy the beauty of the hill-girt horizon as seen from the house.

Thawing comfortably before the fire, Phyllis pursued her train of thought: "I wish Alethea could sleep with me instead of in the tower."

"It's her Ladyship's orders, dear."

It was remarkable that for all practical purposes the running of the huge house and the comfort of its inmates depended solely on the three upper servants, butler, house-keeper and cook. When visitors were expected Lady Vayne said who was coming and where they were to sleep; this very capable trio did the rest. Truelove the butler—

or steward as he preferred to be called—might be said to form the base of the triangle, but whereas the other two parts were equal to each other, neither was quite equal to him. The friendliest relations existed between Truelove and Monsieur Pérez, whom the steward did not regard as a rival. Temperamental like most artists, the chef seldom left his great kitchen, preferring the privacy of his cubby-hole partitioned off from the kitchen proper and furnished with a writing-table and two easy chairs. Here Truelove would sometimes visit him, and sometimes, but more rarely, the chef visited the steward in his panelled sitting-room, also opening off the cloisters and known, as distinct from the housekeeper's room, simply as 'the Room.'

Friendly relations also existed between the chef and Mrs. Campbell, but between her and Truelove nothing more than an uneasy neutrality and all the suspicion and jealousy which two strong personalities both highly competent could engender; but whereas the housekeeper never interfered in the steward's domain, he could and did frequently interfere in hers.

"I'm having a very pretty dress for the play," Mrs. Campbell's young visitor, now sprawling at ease in a chair on the opposite side of the hearth, remarked. "It's pale blue satin, long, right down to my feet, with a waist high up under my arms."

"Yes, dear, I saw it to-day in the workroom—Miss Pont showed it me."

Pont, Lady Vayne's maid, was an accomplished dress-maker. To see her fitting a skirt with at least half a dozen pins in her mouth was to know one was watching a crafts-woman. Nevertheless, it was useless to pretend that a coat made by Pont was the same as one made by a tailor—even a local one.

"Alethea's dress has a bright red skirt and a velvet bodice with spangles, lacing up like a pair of stays, only in front," continued Phyllis. "And she's to wear a handkerchief on her head. I've got a straw hat with little pink rosebuds. Mama's going to have a great curly white wig and Lettice too. Hilda's to have two dresses; isn't she lucky? I think I know all my part perfectly except the long bit at the end. I wish I hadn't got to sing though. Wasn't it awful that time when I was quite little and started in the wrong key?"

"I don't remember that, Miss Phyllis. You always did act beautifully and sing, too, even as quite a little girl. How we all enjoyed it last year! Her Ladyship looked so beautiful. She might have been trained for the stage—she acts so natural."

This was true—Lady Vayne and her brother were the star performers in the Vyne Theatrical Company.

Phyllis was warm again and ready to go upstairs.

Her hat hanging by its elastic on the back of her neck, she paused on her way to the door to survey the decked tea-table, where a lavish assortment of scones, crumpets, sandwiches, cakes and jams was set out.

"Do tell Anna not to send up that cherry cake for our tea again to-day. I hate cherry cake. Can't we have a seed one?"

"You and your old seed cake! There's nobody but you and Sir Thomas as ever touches it!" The housekeeper was scornful but indulgent. "You'd better be quick then and tell Anna at once; your tea must be just going up. Oh— and as you're going up, dear, ask Sarah to come down and speak to me a minute; she'll be in the housemaids' cupboard."

Skipping into the conveniently adjoining still-room, Phyllis found Anna the still-room maid and George the hall-boy in the act of loading his tray with the school-room tea, including the hated cherry cake. Poor George was the servant of the servants, and besides waiting on them he frequently did their work as well as his own. Mrs. Campbell seated beside her fire, a full coal-scuttle within reach, would not hesitate to ring her bell summoning him from his work at the opposite end of the house to make up the fire for her. Yet no ill-feeling was aroused. The victim accepted it as being quite in order, for the upper servants had all been through the same mill. If he managed to grow tall enough he would in time become a footman, perhaps eventually attain to such a position as Mr. Truelove's.

Quickly setting them right over the cherry cake, Phyllis proceeded up the back stairs, also conveniently adjoining the still-room. In the days of Elizabeth, even service stair-cases were beautiful. This was of dark oak throughout with newel posts topped by pierced finials. Strong oaken planks running the length of each flight took the place of balustrading.

Halfway up in the 'cupboard,' which was really a fair-sized room and always smelt of yellow soap and beeswax, Sarah, the head housemaid, was singing at the sink, beside her a large array of brightly polished brass hot-water cans ready for the visitors' bedrooms. She knew better than to disregard the housekeeper's summons, and started immediately downstairs whilst Phyllis continued up. On the top floor the staircase ended in a long corridor lit by windows looking on to the central court and running round three sides of the house. The fourth was occupied by the Long Gallery.

Down this passage Phyllis hurried, through a door separating the back premises from the grand staircase, and

The Long Gallery

so to the end of the passage and the door of the Long Gallery, through which came sounds of hammering.

A stage had been built at this end of the gallery and on it as expected she found Jim Bowden, the house-carpenter, putting the final touches to the woodland scene where the action of the play was set. Seen from the lighted stage, the great length of the dark gallery seemed to stretch away into infinity. To Phyllis it looked a little ghostly and frightening, but no more so than was pleasant.

The walls were covered to within three feet of the

ceiling with Tudor panelling. Halfway down the outer wall the huge chimney-piece, stone and gilded plaster, with the arms of Elizabeth in the centre, reached to the ceiling. On either side of this a row of long, uncurtained windows now showed only a deep purple twilight outside, and the two at the end looking on to the forecourt were almost invisible from the stage.

Surveying the completed woodland scene which had been specially painted for the occasion, Phyllis thought it wonderful; the path winding away into the trees on the backcloth looked as if by a slight effort of will it could be walked upon. There was a fine drop curtain, too (which was up at the moment), showing the house surmounting its buttresses, with the Italian garden in the foreground below. They were doing a gipsy play this year. She was to be the rich young lady in love with a poor young man whom her worldly-minded guardian would not allow her to marry. The gipsies would help to circumvent him and true love triumph in the end. Last year she had been the beautiful village maiden courted by the wicked Duke (her brother Richard) and the virtuous peasant boy (her other brother, Piers). At one point in the play Piers had to say: "I am a poor but honest peasant"; and the Duke to reply: "A poor but honest pheasant! I will shoot you, you miserable pheasant!" "No, you cannot shoot me till October!" Of course, the audience had not failed to go into the appropriate roars of laughter. After this there was to be a highwayman piece in which her mother and Uncle William took the leading roles. Her sister Lettice was to play opposite Captain Tarporley, the son of a neighbouring squire, and rehearsals were to start on Boxing Day. The producer and manager was to be

Mr. Blunt, who was by no means easy to please and something of a perfectionist.

Her father never took part in the acting. Though always ready to acclaim their success, he could be counted on to throw plenty of cold water at the outset. In fact, Sir Thomas Vayne either pretended to or really did dislike Christmas and all its festivities, unbelievable as this seemed to his youngest daughter. Phyllis had even noticed a slight tendency on the part of Lettice and Richard to be a little blasé about it also. Sometimes Richard seemed to forget about this, but if it awoke in her too violent a response he would very quickly revert to his former mood.

She now put her request to Jim, which was that he should make them a sham chicken for the supper scene in the play. Jim Bowden, a small man with a large, drooping moustache, seemed dubious.

"Mr. Truelove said as 'ow 'e thought you could make do with a real one," he replied at last.

At this moment the door at the far end of the gallery started to creak open, and gradually emerging from the darkness into the rays of the footlights a group of men appeared bearing a large fir tree. Slowly and carefully they advanced accompanied by a tall commanding figure which took no share of the burden but directed them at every step. At its orders they placed the tree about halfway down the room and some way in front of the stage.

"That will do, thank you."

Truelove, for it was he, dismissed the gardeners and turned to Phyllis, who had left the stage to inspect the tree.

It would have been hard to find a more perfect butler

than Truelove. He was tall, but not quite so tall as his footmen, and that was as it should be. Immaculate in appearance, rigidly upright, quiet, dignified, confident, there was one thing about him both unconventional and surprising in a butler: his upper lip was closely shaved, but his lower jaw was covered by a grey growth, perfectly kept and trimmed and not unlike King Edward's, but still a beard. ·

There was a rumour that Truelove had a delicate throat which must be protected, but the more probable explanation was that it placed him above the general level, gave him a particular cachet. What Mr. Brown of Bayswater could not tolerate in his butler, Sir Thomas Vayne of Vyne could and did. So Truelove had a beard.

"A nice tree, don't you think, miss?" he now remarked to Phyllis.

"Oh yes, but it's not quite such a good shape as last year's."

"Ah, wait till I've tied on a few extra branches. Jim, come over here please, I want you."

And taking the hint, Phyllis left to get ready for tea.

Truelove was always at his best at Christmas. It gave him a chance to go all out and display to the full his powers of organisation. It was as if he said: "We'll show them what Vyne can do!" Or perhaps more truly: "What I can do with Vyne." The tree was his responsibility and no one else was allowed to decorate it. When the children of the estate employees came up on Boxing Day to have tea and receive their presents it was he who acted as master of ceremonies. After tea in the servants' hall, lit for the occasion with Chinese lanterns, they would troop upstairs to the Long Gallery, where the tree in all its glory for the second day in succession provided, except for the blazing fire, the only light in the room. Ready and waiting, rather behind Truelove, Jim Bowden and Gregory the plumber would stand with sponges on the ends of long sticks. Then when everyone had walked round the tree and admired it thoroughly, Truelove would read out from a list, not the children's names but their parents' names and their respective ages—a nice distinction.

"Jim Bowden's little girl, aged six years"—and a small girl in best frock and button boots would clatter across the shiny boards to where Lady Vayne stood beside the tree, receive her gift with a bobbed curtsey and clatter back again.

"George Jackson's little boy, aged six years"—the same ceremony again, till from the youngest to the eldest they had all had their presents. Then Truelove would make a speech.

It was the same every year—"I'm sure we're all very grateful to her Ladyship for providing this beautiful tree and presents. When I was a boy and Christmas came round I was pleased if I got a monkey on a stick. But of course times have changed. Now I want you all to give three hearty cheers," etc.

There was always a loyal response. Then the gallery would resound to the blowing of tin trumpets and whistles, the clicking of pistols and popping of crackers, and the broad North Country accents of excited young voices.

In her own room Phyllis found a cheerful fire and a can of hot water (but not a brass one) standing in the

[15]

wash-basin covered by a towel. On the bed lay a white muslin frock for her to change into after tea, and on the chest of drawers done up in white paper her little contribution of Christmas presents.

She never quite knew how she managed to collect the money to pay for these. Nominally she received a shilling a week pocket money from her father, but he was not always there or sometimes could not be bothered, so she had to wait a favourable opportunity and get several weeks' at a time. Sometimes this worked to her advantage.

This year she had knitted him a silk necktie and it had cost her nothing, as her mother had paid for the silk. For her governess she had a pair of woollen mittens, also her own work and knitted at her mother's expense. For Lettice, her eldest sister, she had a handkerchief sachet scented with lavender, and for Richard a framed photograph of Mike the Irish terrier taken by herself. For Piers there was a penknife, and for Hilda, the one nearest her own age, a book by L. T. Meade. Her mother's present was always the most costly and was a joint offering from all of them. Lettice had chosen it, a Georgian snuffbox, and it had cost a whole pound.

The fortunate Lettice always accompanied her parents when they went to London for the three weeks before Christmas. If only, thought Phyllis, she might have gone too, for just long enough to do her shopping at Harrods; delectable Harrods with its moving staircase, the ornate plaster work on walls and ceilings, its heavy bosses and curlicues, so reminiscent of iced cakes, almost made her mouth water. And just inside the main entrance, in the Stationery, that exquisite little red-leather covered

folding writing-table, equipped with every possible acces-
sory from patent inkstand, pens and sealing wax to per-
petual calendar, paper and penknife. What a glorious
Christmas present for anybody! But, of course, beyond
her wildest dreams. Failing the writing-table, however,
what an infinite choice of lesser objects more suited to
her purse lay disposed on every side. Instead, she and
Hilda had to make do with the village shop, not as yet,
but later, renamed the 'Gifte Shoppe,' which dealt ex-
clusively in 'novelties and fancy goods,' and they would
devote a whole afternoon to it, the coachman having to
put up at the Vayne Arms. Although their combined expenditure amounted to less than a sovereign, kind Mrs.
Turner would give them her undivided attention whilst
they pored over her stock-in-trade; china cats with
elongated necks, coy shepherds and shepherdesses,
'trinket' stands and inkstands which might have been
expressly designed to defeat their own ends, being wide
at the rim and tiny at the base, satin cushions and night-
dress cases painted with flowers, small trumpet-shaped
silver vases at the very sight of which any flower might
be expected to wither and die—such was the composition
of the supply base from which Christmas after Christmas
the two youngest Vaynes had to make their selections.

Hilda was having tea at the vicarage this evening, a
rather rare invitation which for some reason had not been
extended to her younger sister. A better mixer than Phyllis,
Hilda was a great favourite at the mothers' meeting, which
held weekly sessions throughout the autumn and winter.
Lettice had lately emancipated herself from attendance at
these meetings, but Lady Vayne, quite determined not to
suffer alone, always insisted on one or both of her younger

daughters accompanying her. For Phyllis it was certainly an ordeal, especially on a fine afternoon when she might have been on the moors or golf course. The only advantage was that it meant rather less time at afternoon lessons. It was not permissible to knit things like silk ties at the meeting—only woollen garments, socks or scarves known as 'comforters' were allowed. They met in the upper room of a disused public house on the outskirts of the village, perched at the top of so steep a hill that they had to get out of the carriage and walk up the last stretch of the lane. Invariably they were met at the summit by old Mrs. Swindells, the mother-in-chief, ceaselessly plying her steel knitting needles even as she came to greet them. In appearance she was the stock witch of Grimm's fairy stories—every feature perfect—mournful heavy-lidded eyes gazing fixedly from under a deeply corrugated brow, great curved nose almost meeting the sharp, jutting chin, and in between the sunken crescent of a mouth, devoid of even a single tooth. Only the high-crowned hat was replaced by a large black bonnet, and her expression was lugubrious rather than wicked.

She seemed to draw her soul's sustenance from receiving and transmitting bad news:

"Mrs. Gee's 'ad another narsty fall. Broke 'er leg. Doctor says she won't never wark agen.

"It's a pity about Mr. Jackson. 'Aven't you 'eard? 'E died larst night!

"It was 'is broother as 'oong 'imself in bedroom, soomer before larst. Wife's bin in asylum ever since."

Phyllis's spirits would sink lower and lower as she and Hilda followed their mother and Mrs. Swindells out of the fresh air into the dark building, up the narrow stairs and into the stuffy room with the large coal fire in the hob grate and every window closed. There would be a scraping of chairs as the gathering of middle-aged and elderly women (there was hardly ever a young face to be seen) rose respectfully at Lady Vayne's entrance. She and her daughters had to sit at a small table facing the gathering, with their backs to the large fire. The proceedings began with a chapter from some suitable book, possibly one of Mrs. Humphry Ward's—and this was the time when the knitting for the charitable society was done. After about twenty minutes the book was abandoned and hymns chosen by the mothers from the Moody and Sankey collection would be sung, Lady Vayne playing the accompaniment on a cracked piano. Almost always the hymns included ' Jesus wants me for a sunbeam.'

After that there would be a chapter from the Bible and then roll-call: "Martha Whittaker?" "Yes, m'lady." "Elizabeth Gaskell?" "Yes, m'lady." "Ellen Rowbottom?" "Yes, m'lady." "Mary Wild?" "Not here, m'lady."

Phyllis always hoped the owner of this name would be present. It seemed to hold out promise of somebody young and interesting—but never once did Mary Wild put in an appearance. After roll-call the meeting broke up.

Phyllis knew she was not a success with the mothers who, of course, guessed she was an unwilling participant. "Ah, I like Miss 'ilda!" said one matron looking pointedly at Phyllis, who with difficulty could complete only two woollen comforters in the season, whilst Hilda's pile of assorted garments would have done credit to a much older person. Yet they themselves seemed to be in two minds as to the undiluted pleasure of the meetings, for once when Lady Vayne was apologising for not being able to come the following week, "Beg pardon, m'lady," said one of them, "but next week's Wakes week—and we always have a holiday in Wakes week."

When ready for tea, Phyllis passed into the adjoining schoolroom, where she found both her German governess and tea waiting.

Fräulein Thur, who only left her pupils during the summer holidays, was rather remarkable in that she spoke German, French and English almost equally well. Rigidly conscientious, she never allowed a word of English to pass between her and her pupils except during the Christmas holidays or when visitors were present. She and Phyllis spent most of their time together and on the whole got on well, for Fräulein Thur (in spite of her protests she was always called 'Fräulein') had a kind heart. She was rather elderly and summer or winter never wore anything but black. Above her broad Dutch doll's face her greying hair was arranged in two conical puffs rising like twin volcanoes from a centre parting.

"*Liebes kind,* where have you been since you left me?" she asked. "I saw your father in the garden; he was looking for you to go with him to feed the ducks."

Sir Thomas had an almost passionate love for birds. Rare and decorative waterfowl, teal, widgeon, pintail and gorgeous mandarins graced the ornamental lake which bounded the lawn and sometimes nested on its banks. Demoiselle and crested cranes from South America and gold and silver pheasants haunted the glades of the wood and water-garden, and a peculiar species of ostrich, a rather bad-tempered pair, stalked the lime avenue at the back of the house. The climate was too severe to allow many of these creatures to breed; but if any of them ever did produce offspring there was great rejoicing, and corresponding black gloom if they did not survive. Phyllis thought secretly that her father's love of birds was the real reason why he never now made one of the guns at a shoot. Rather ironically, though born to great possessions, he was a man of simple tastes and unconventional ideas, for whom life in the grand manner had no appeal. He carried his dislike of any kind of display or vulgarity to such lengths that his wife once said of him that he would be content to dress in rags if it would not make him too conspicuous. More far-seeing than many, he often said places like Vyne were an incubus and to live in them a mistake. Life in a villa by the sea would be infinitely preferable, and in fact he predicted most of them would so be living before they were much older. To Lettice, who in London was not allowed out walking unaccompanied, he had said: "You ought to be going about in buses alone." He much preferred parlourmaids to 'great stupid louts of footmen' and would have liked to introduce them at Vyne.

But Lady Vayne did not share these views. She was quite determined that neither should Lettice frequent buses with or without her maid, nor parlourmaids be seen whisking their streamers and aprons about the stately rooms of Vyne. She had no yearnings for villa life whether by the sea or elsewhere. Vyne was what she wanted and she loved it with a wholehearted, almost passionate devotion, later to find expression in a real labour of love—a history of the house and family from its foundation. Compiled from a mass of ancient documents (her own discovery) this work was to receive recognition as a valuable contribution to the history of English country life.

Phyllis, who felt just the same as her mother about their home, was sometimes troubled by a question she longed to put but was doubtful if anybody knew the answer. Hilda was the only person she had approached on the subject, and she had frankly confessed herself unable to make a pronouncement.

The question was: when, as she hoped, one at last reached heaven, would one find Vyne there? She had no doubt whatever of what her mother would reply—it would be yes—most decidedly; in fact, Phyllis knew that for her mother heaven was unimaginable without Vyne. But did her mother really know? Fräulein she also had no doubt would reply differently. Life in heaven would far transcend any earthly form of happiness, but if it were possible on that plane to experience pleasure in things and places as on earth, then they would be more like the things and places in Germany. Canon Waldegrave, their parish priest, Phyllis felt ought to know, but she was far too shy to ask him, so the question remained unanswered.

Fräulein Thur understood her small pupil better than anyone else. She knew her weaknesses and her good points. Like all her family she was shy and reserved but in addition selfconscious and rather vain—anxious to excel but at the same time both lazy and diffident: good-hearted and generous in some things, tiresomely self-assertive and too easily roused to anger in others. She had the excuse of extreme youth. There were, however, as with all human relationships, things both good and bad in Phyllis of which her governess knew nothing.

She was too excited to eat much tea although her

favourite seed cake was on the table, and she soon asked Fräulein's permission to leave her and go downstairs. Mike the terrier was waiting by the door and slipped out as she opened it. He always appeared with schoolroom tea, remained while they had it and took his share, but nothing would induce him to stay one minute after it was cleared away, and if possible, as now, he left before. For this reason Phyllis could never feel any great affection for Mike.

Back in her own room she scrambled into the muslin frock and tied the sash as best she could, which was not very well. Louisa, the French maid she shared with Lettice and Hilda, would still be at her tea, especially as some visiting maids would have arrived by now, and it would be a shame to ring for her. Tea for the upper servants was always served in the housekeeper's room, 'the Room' being reserved for the more solid meals. It was from 'the Room' that the procession headed by Truelove and Mrs. Campbell started, making its way round the cloisters to the servants' hall, there to eat the first course of meat and vegetables with the underlings in perfect silence. Then, again in procession and doubtless to the great relief of 'the Hall,' back they went to finish the rest of the meal in 'the Room.' Here Phyllis had been told Truelove made himself very pleasant to the ladies and no doubt they had great fun, as additional male society was provided by Withers, Sir Thomas's valet, and any visiting valets who happened to come. Mrs. Campbell was scornful of Truelove's conversational powers—"Tales one's 'eard over and over again," was how she described them, but this opinion was not shared by the ladies' maids.

A few years ago when Lettice was still in the

schoolroom, and Richard at his private school, they would all on occasion be invited to tea in 'the Room,' and there were few things more enjoyable. In the first place, the tea, at which Truelove presided, was of the most sumptuous and luscious kind, with unusual things like shrimps and sardines, and of course, crackers. Also 'the Room' itself was so delightful with its Tudor panelling and chimney-piece, just like the one in the Long Gallery—it certainly added to the enjoyment. After tea they played games with forfeits, Truelove again taking charge; Withers, Mrs. Campbell and the ladies' maids were allowed to be present and joined in the games. It was all the greatest fun, and Phyllis much regretted that these happy parties were now things of the past.

She knew her grandmother was arriving earlier than the others and also, she thought, Cousin Amy, a great favourite at Vyne and without whom no Christmas party was complete. They would be having tea in the saloon, so down the passage she ran again, through the door at the top of the grand staircase and down it to the first floor where all the principal rooms were placed.

Here, as on the floor above, a passage ran round three sides of the central court, the entrance hall filling the fourth. The staircase, late seventeenth century with classical balustrading, rose from a side hall with rectangular oak pillars at one end of which was the door of the library, at the other that of the saloon. A year ago the huge house was still lit entirely by oil lamps. On the staircase they had stood precariously balanced on the broad tops of the newel posts at each turn of the stairs. It was a marvel there had never been a catastrophe. Now a large electric chandelier flinging its powerful lights upwards brightly

illumined the family portraits covering the staircase walls
—Elizabethan Sir Piers between his two wives: Dame
Margaret, a tall full-length in yellow hooped skirt, long,
narrow bodice and triple strand, knee-length pearl neck-
lace; Dame Dorothy, rather tight-lipped, in severely
tailored black, large white ruff, small, high-crowned hat,
her pet monkey on her lap, and her predecessor's pearls.
On the end wall hung the huge picture of Thomas Vayne,
traveller and Egyptologist, friend of the Prince Regent
(who had condescended to borrow money from him), in
eastern dress, his hand on his horse's neck, his Arab
servant squatting beside him. He it was who had committed the atrocity of the tower and several other vanda-
lisms, but to his credit stood the fine late Georgian
dining-room and the Orangery, which despite its glass
roof had managed to achieve beauty.

Just as Phyllis reached the first floor a tall figure in grey
emerged from the lower level mounting the short flight
of stairs from the entrance hall three steps at a time. Mr.
Blunt also had arrived early.

"Phyllis—my only joy! Why weren't you there to
greet me when I arrived? Closeted with old Gruffenough,
I suppose. Come and kiss your Uncle Blunt."

Catching both her hands in his, Mr. Blunt was about to
greet her affectionately, but drew back with a start of
surprise.

"Great heavens, child—your hands are like nutmeg-
graters! It must be because you don't dry them properly.
Yes—look! They're nothing like properly dried."

So that was why her hands were so chapped that to put
the glycerine jelly on at night was pure agony. Blushing
furiously and mumbling something unintelligible, Phyllis

snatched her hands away. She knew she always hurried too much over her toilet, but to be told about it by Mr. Blunt or anybody but Fräulein or Louisa was humiliating. Shrugging his shoulders, Mr. Blunt opened the library door and closed it behind him, whilst Phyllis fled in the opposite direction towards the saloon.

The door of the saloon opened on a scene of almost unreal loveliness; not the unreality of a stage setting, much more like an exquisite dream—a scene of comfort, elegance, beauty, not quite of this world. It was a large, lofty room with walls of darkly glowing cedar-wood, Corinthian pilasters arranged in pairs dividing the long panels and each of these adorned down its centre with swags of elaborate wood-carvings. From looped garlands and palm leaves and cupids' heads hung a host of diverse objects, bunches of fruit and flowers, musical instruments, trophies, fish and birds, all carved to the life in soft yellow pear-wood by the hand of the master—the one and only Grinling Gibbons. The ceiling was decorated with gilt scroll-work of Italian design, and from its centre like a great golden flower the carved wood chandelier spread its aura around. From standards and wall brackets artfully shaded with mother-of-pearl a constellation of lesser lights added its lustre and the whole reflected in glasses and polished panelling made the room seem to be enveloped in a haze of gold. Over the three long windows curtains of bright yellow damask shimmered and scintillated in the lights and melted in the shadows to a clear, translucent green. Above them curved the gilt plumes and arabesques of fantastically carved canopies. Opposite the door a glass large enough to reflect three-fourths of the scene gave just a suggestion of magic to the room and its contents: inlaid, ormolu-mounted commodes whose marble tops held pieces of old Dresden and Chelsea china ; bureaux and tables with spiral legs; an ancient harpsichord and high-backed Queen Anne chairs all of pale yellow walnut. A tall leather screen painted with

flowers and birds protected the sofa where Lady Vayne sat beside her mother, and on the other side of the hearth, with its blazing fire in a cut steel grate, Lettice, on a Queen Anne settee, sat talking to Cousin Amy.

Dividing the actual room from the one in the looking-glass rose a hedge of chrysanthemums, scarlet poinsettias and lilies. Elsewhere stood pots of fuchsias and gloxinias. There were long-branching, many-coloured carnations and small, clustering, bright pink begonias, and on one table two or three lilies of the arum family shaped like scarlet parasols with long yellow spikes, standing up stiffly in a tall vase.

A little shyly Phyllis advanced to kiss her grandmother, who was so frail she had to be treated like a piece of china.

"Ah, here's little Phyllis! How are you, darling?"

The gentle old voice was very broken and croaky, but the speaker still had great beauty; looking at her one could see the Lady Vayne of years to come. On her head she wore a graceful arrangement of lace which might have been called a cap but was more like a mantilla, and under it her still plentiful grey hair was charmingly arranged.

Grandmamma, thought Phyllis as she kissed her, always smelt like babies, of violet powder and orris root.

Unconsciously tactless, she turned with obviously greater pleasure to greet Cousin Amy, who was always so jolly—never had she been known to say a cross word and her store of amusing anecdotes was seemingly inexhaustible. It was a pity she could not be spared from the piano to take a part in the play.

Lettice soon noticed Phyllis's badly tied sash and started tweaking it into shape. Cousin Amy wanted to know all about the play and whether Phyllis knew her part. She had found a very pretty song, she said, which, if Mr. Blunt approved, ought to fit perfectly into the play and would not be difficult to sing. Lettice said rather caustically that would be a good thing, and she hoped it was a short one. Phyllis blushed and looked awkward.

"Never mind, darling," said her mother, "you'll do it all right."

"That child's grown," said Grandmamma, who was sometimes a trifle obvious.

Withers came in with Charles, the second footman, to remove the tea-table, which with all its equipment of silver and eatables still stood in front of the sofa; Truelove, of course, was busy with the tree. Quickly, deftly, noiselessly they removed it and withdrew.

"You're sure you're not tired after your long drive, Mamma darling?" Lady Vayne enquired tenderly of her mother. The long drive had been twelve miles in her closed carriage from the neighbouring estate, where she still reigned as châtelaine with her bachelor son. It was from here that her eldest daughter had come as a girl to marry young Thomas Vayne of Vyne.

"Don't you think you ought to go to your room and rest?"

But, emphasising each word with a narrow, long-fingered hand: "Not tired at all," said Grandmamma, "not tired at *all*."

"Come and hold my skein of wool for me, Babbles," said Lady Vayne, who was knitting a pair of stockings for Richard.

How could she sit so calmly winding wool, thought Phyllis, taking her place on the footstool beside her mother's chair, when they were on the verge of such delirious excitements; and the crowd of visitors on the point of arriving. Even now they might be on their way up from the station. Ruggles, the coachman, had gone to meet them with the horse-drawn omnibus, and Cullen, the under-coachman (now the chauffeur), with the new Daimler, which he had only just learnt to drive. They might at this moment be disembarking at the entrance porch, with John the hall-porter and the footmen waiting for them and Truelove escorting them across the courtyard and up the steps into the hall. There they would only pause long enough to take off their overcoats before coming up the short flight of steps to the first floor, and some of the men of the party might go straight into the library, but most of them would come in here. One could not hear a sound, but they might be coming now. At that instant the opening of the door and the sound of clumping boots on the polished boards made her jump up. But it was only Richard with Cousin Harry, who must have arrived with Mr. Blunt and been all this time in private session with Richard.

The boys were at school together, Harry being slightly the elder. Exclamations of pleasure at the appearance of this young male contingent came from the sofa, decidedly more so than when Phyllis had made her entry. Did Harry want tea? Should she have it brought back? his aunt wanted to know. But Harry thanked her and said no, he had had tea at Crewe. Lady Vayne's fond gaze never left her son as the boys came forward to pay their respects to the ladies. No doubt she was thinking what was perfectly obvious, that he was the better looking of the two. Their clothes were much alike, but Richard wore his with a difference, an easy grace which belonged to him.

Phyllis had once heard her father say with the nonchalant air which masked his pride: "Richard could do anything," and judging solely from her own experience she felt this was true.

Sir Thomas took no interest in the Turf and owned no racehorses; there was no hunting within twenty miles of Vyne and there was hardly an acre in the entire park where thanks to the rabbits it was not perilous to gallop a horse, so perhaps for these reasons and lack of encouragement they were not a horsy family; but with this rather surprising exception, Richard seemed to have a natural aptitude for all forms of sport. He could shoot almost as well as Uncle William. He could throw a fly better than his father. He drove a longer ball at golf than anybody except the professional who lived in the village and sometimes played with them on the hilly nine-hole course in the park. All Phyllis knew of the game she had learnt from Richard, and he had taught her with patience and skill, giving encouragement as well as criticism. He took wonderful photographs with his German camera which he developed himself and showed her how to develop her own. He had in addition a pretty wit, and for Phyllis his judgment upon people and things was final.

It was not yet decided what career Richard was to adopt. Sir Thomas was for Diplomacy, Uncle William for Parliament, Lady Vayne for the Guards. Richard himself kept an open mind. There was plenty of time anyhow, as he was still only in his middle teens.

For different reasons which to him seemed valid, Sir Thomas was also proud of all his other children, in particular of his eldest for her shrewd judgment and

perception and her already marked success with the opposite sex, and of his youngest, perhaps only because she *was*
the youngest, and, as she herself was well aware, with little
cause, for her intelligence. Even now she sometimes felt
hot remembering times when he had tried to draw her
out in front of visitors and how her efforts to respond
must have appeared to outsiders not blinded by paternal
love. In fact, this was the only instance when Sir Thomas
might have been accused of a slight tendency to show off.
Fräulein sometimes felt it necessary to warn Phyllis that
her father was not an impartial judge and that far from
being of a quick intelligence she was rather slow of
understanding. Sometimes Sir Thomas's ardent wish to
prove his child's ability took the form of general knowledge questions at meals, and this was agonising. He
would suddenly ask—"Who was Cordelia?" or "What
are the principal rivers of China?" or still worse some
question in mental arithmetic. Sometimes Lady Vayne
would intervene and protect her, but only too often she
was occupied with someone at the other end of the table.
Then Phyllis would have to struggle unaided, conscious
of Fräulein at her side furiously indignant at her pupil's
failure to do her credit. But, of course, nothing like this
ever happened in the Christmas holidays.

Lady Vayne did not go all the way with her husband
where her daughters were concerned, but even she de-
ferred to Lettice's judgment. One afternoon proposing
they should drive over to visit an elderly couple who
lived in a ghostly old house supposed to be haunted by
several spectres, including that of Charles I, Lettice had
said: "Oh, don't let's go—it's so dreadfully boring visiting the old Hampdens," and Lady Vayne though a little

annoyed had given way. A trifling matter, but considering the general ascendancy of mothers over daughters in those times it was significant.

The door was opening again and this time there was a chorus of welcome from the whole room, for it was Uncle William accompanied by Piers who had been waiting about for his arrival. Responding joyfully he entered and was taken into the heart of the company and of the saloon.

Following quickly upon his entrance came the big rush of arrivals, including Aunt Lucy and Uncle Andrew, Hilda just returned from the vicarage, and the person most welcome to Phyllis, her cousin Alethea.

Alethea was about Phyllis's age and her great friend. They did much the same things and wore the same kind of clothes, but as with Richard and his boy cousin, they looked different, for Alethea was a beauty. Her hair curled naturally, she had regular features and lovely colouring, the grace of her body and its every movement were a delight to watch, but as if this were not enough, she was also blessed with a natural charm of manner deriving from an almost total lack of shyness or selfconsciousness. Now, whilst eager to get Alethea to herself, Phyllis knew she must wait until the grown-ups had paid that tribute in the form of attention which exceptional beauty always receives. And very wonderfully Alethea still received it, with complete modesty and lack of conceit.

Just for a moment a detached observer gazing over the heads of chrysanthemums and lilies into the depths of the glass where the whole scene was reproduced, a strange feeling took possession of Phyllis.

The group round the sofa, the other by the settee, the

The Saloon

standing figures round the fire, the flowering lights of the chandelier, the whole room and its occupants seemed like a dream, transient and fleeting, from which she would soon wake to a cold, unpleasant reality. A little shudder ran through her, but turning quickly from the mirror to the actual scene, she was at once immersed again in her warm sea of happiness. No cold breath could reach her. It was real all right, this golden moment, with the people she loved in the place she adored, her beautiful, wonderful home, and it seemed to be going to last for ever.

In due course her patience was rewarded. The grown-ups relinquished Alethea and the two little girls were soon excitedly chattering together.

"Alethea, do you know your part? I know all mine. You must come and see the woodland scene to-night. It's the best we've ever had. And your dress is lovely and so's mine."

Alethea confessed she was not quite sure of all her words, but as her part was smaller than Phyllis's she would soon learn it. Would they be dining down to-night? No, not till to-morrow night. And here Uncle William strolled over and joined them.

Of all the grown-ups he entered most whole-heartedly into the Christmas revels. He loved them because he not only loved children but was a child himself at heart. When he played a childish game he was not indifferent if he won or lost. He went all out to win and was not too proud to show regret if he did not. Perhaps he was at his best with little girls. Now he came up to them saying: "Hullo, you two, what's this I hear about you spending to-morrow evening with Fräulein playing question and

[35]

answer in German and not coming down to dinner?" They both shouted at him in delighted protest, and Alethea, of course, was ready with a neat repartee. His humour was of the obvious kind which delights children, never above their heads and impossible to misunderstand.

A Christmas or two ago at luncheon, with the table stretching from end to end of the big dining-room Phyllis had secured the coveted place by his side; a pink sugar-coated sweet was being handed round bearing the words 'Bonne Année' in white letters. He had said to her, "Look! that's Boney Annie," and she had chuckled with delight, particularly because at that time she was not too sure what 'Bonne Année' meant when she saw it written; and after it had been some way round the table he had said, "Annie looks more boney than ever now."

There came a sudden burst of laughter from the group round the fire. One of the new arrivals, a young man named Clive in his second year at Oxford, was the cause of it. With cries of "Come on now, hand it over," Piers and Harry flung themselves upon him. There was a short scuffle and the thing in question was snatched from his breast-pocket. Triumphantly, Piers held it aloft for all to see—a glossy picture-postcard bearing the head of Miss Gabrielle Ray. But smiling and unperturbed Clive, an unusual young man, clearly enjoyed being the cynosure of all eyes, even though the laughter was more at than with him. Adroitly deflecting attention from the picture-postcard, he launched into an account of the latest romance of stage and society, one so fresh and new that the press gossip-writers had not yet got their teeth into it. A man at his college, the eldest son of a peer, had just engaged himself to one of the Gaiety girls. He had all the details, the girl's name and the reported family reaction to it. They were making a virtue of necessity. "Oh, how furious his mother must be! I know who she wanted him to marry—— What's she like?" the deeply interested Lettice questioned eagerly. But here Clive failed badly. He had to admit that he had not even seen, much less met, the girl. Anyhow at this point he was robbed of his audience.

The door opened once more and this time it was True-love coming to announce to Lady Vayne that the men were ready and waiting downstairs. This was the signal for the ritual which took place at Vyne every Christmas Eve, and instantly Lady Vayne rose, beckoned her children and, followed by those members of the house party who wished to attend, left the saloon.

They paused at the door of the library to collect Sir Thomas, who was there talking to Mr. Blunt and Lord Belgrave, a political friend who had just arrived; and thus augmented, the party descended to the hall level, filed through a door at the head of the pantry stairs and down them to the kitchen. This was situated in the south-east corner of the cloisters where the pavement took a gradual downward slope and the fourth wall of the courtyard became a vaulted passage connecting the kitchen with the servants' hall. Off this again ran another subterranean passage with brushing rooms opening off it, where Withers and the footmen did the valeting and cleaned the boots. Still beyond, running at right angles to it, was the cavernous tunnel leading to the brew house and wine cellars and the steep flight of steps which at last emerged into the light of day, nearly two hundred yards from the centre of the house. No one knew how old these passages were; some said they dated from Edward VI or even earlier and that still further under the hillside ran another tunnel which emerged at last at the old square tower known as the Cage. Within living memory coal had been dug from these caverns until it became unsafe to continue doing so. Now the family used the tunnel on wet days to get to the stables, where Sir Thomas had converted some of the loose boxes into a squash-racquet court.

To-night a double row of waiting figures stood facing each other in the vaulted passage between the kitchen and the servants' hall, extending down its entire length.

In the kitchen there was a scene of orderly bustle, Pérez and his maids passing to and fro across the stone-flagged floor preparing dinner, chopping, stirring, mixing, pounding, without heeding the influx from above stairs. Cotton, the bailiff, and Mottram, the shepherd, in one of Pérez's white aprons, were waiting, and Lady Vayne took her place at a small table, her family ranging themselves behind her. Along the shelves of the huge dresser in front of the rows of gleaming copper, innumerable joints of raw beef, each bearing a label, were laid out. Truelove by the door held a list in his hand from which, just as he did at the Christmas tree party, he proceeded to read out names. Then, one after another, each man employed on the estate entered, advanced to the table and spread out a huge cotton handkerchief, the shepherd dumped a joint of beef upon it and Lady Vayne, gathering up the corners, just, but only just, succeeded in knotting them over the joint. Having done this, she wished the recipient a happy Christmas and received his good wishes in return. The business took about an hour.

They came in strict order of precedence. The coachman, the head gardener, the clerk of the works, the head keeper: this last a very striking figure.

He came in rather slowly on his rheumaticky old legs, a bearded giant in a green tail coat and corduroy breeches and gaiters, the garb of the Vyne gamekeepers. Jesse Ardern was one of the old guard, just due to retire on a pension, but for all that poachers still kept clear of his preserves. Nevertheless, despite his vigilance and the formidable size of all the keepers, outlying coverts suffered from the periodic maraudings of gangs of poachers. Coming from quite far afield, they took a steady toll of pheasants, black-cock, rabbits and any other available game throughout the year. Many were the hampers despatched by rail to London which found their way to the West End poulterers, who had come to regard these consignments as a valuable source of supply.

Jesse was 'no scholar,' in other words could neither read nor write, and therefore had some difficulty in counting the heads of game at a shoot, but a prodigious memory and powers of observation (there was little that escaped his notice) served him instead. His only drawback was extreme taciturnity. When Lady Vayne visited Mrs. Ardern, as she did periodically the wives of all the employees, Jesse would sometimes put in an appearance, but as Mrs. Ardern was as sparing of words as himself, Lady Vayne had either to sit with them in silence or conduct a monologue.

When Richard was born, Sir Thomas's sister, meeting

Jesse near the kennels, had stopped to comment on the joyful event.

"Well, Jesse, this is splendid news, isn't it?"

"Ah."

"We've wanted this for a long time, haven't we?"

"Ah."

"It's a fine baby, too."

"Ah."

"And the little girl, Miss Lettice, is growing fast."

"Aye."

At this point she gave up.

Victor Emanuel Sidebottom, another gamekeeper, also of huge stature, followed his chief.

Three families, the Arderns, the Gaskells and the Sidebottoms, might be said to form the aristocracy of the Vyne employees, for though many of them held subordinate posts, all had the distinction of having lived and served at Vyne for many generations. The Sidebottoms, including several variations on the name, amounted almost to a clan. Sidebottoms, Ramsbottoms, Rowbottoms, Shufflebottoms were to be found in almost every department of the estate. Victor Emanuel's son, Albert Edward, was one of the younger gamekeepers, and *his* son, Albert the second, was the kennel boy. A cousin was the blacksmith, another worked on the farm, and another, a distant connection, was employed in the house as odd-man, where amongst his other duties he brewed the beer and cured the hams, but he by decree of Truelove, possibly for brevity's sake, was known as 'Shuffle.' It was the rule of the house that every chance comer, every tradesman, messenger or casual visitor must always be given a drink of this home-brewed beer, one glass of which Mr. Blunt declared was strong enough to put one to sleep for the afternoon.

There were red deer on the moors behind the house and sometimes in the early autumn someone would be sent out to try to kill a stag, Victor Emanuel Sidebottom acting as stalker. But even the best shots were often unsuccessful. When Victor Emanuel moved it was like a small landslide, and too often the marksman crawling behind his mammoth guide was unable to get within range. But the red deer were not confined to the moors. In the hills and valleys of the park, at the edges of the drives, sometimes almost up to the railings of the forecourt, great antlered stags with their numerous wives and families roamed and grazed. In October the sound of their roaring filled the park, and to meet a solitary stag just routed in combat over hinds and fawns was not a pleasant experience. Jock Whittle, a small man with very bowed legs, who walked like a ship in a gale, was said to have spent the whole of one autumn night in a small railed enclosure surrounding a young tree, an angry stag mounting guard over him. He worked on the farm and lived with his wife and son in a tall old house on the edge of the moors. It looked large from the outside but contained only two rooms, one above the other, with the remains of very old mural decoration and a hooded chimney-piece in one. This building appeared in a seventeenth-century picture of Vyne. So also did the Cage. The origin of this strange building was rather obscure. It was believed to have been built in Tudor times by the Sir Piers Vayne who had so transformed the house, but from its size and solidity must have been something more than a watch-tower—probably a place of detention for law-breakers awaiting trial at the county assize. Turner, the park-keeper, lived in this isolated and exposed place, so isolated and exposed that it was not easy to find anyone willing to do so, especially as in addition all the water had to be drawn from a well halfway down the hill. From the roof of the Cage one could see the surrounding country for miles around; on one side the level plain with here and there a distant factory chimney, on the other the wild hill country on the verge of which Vyne was situated, chequered by the grey, dry-stone walls which in those parts took the place of hedges.

The Cage

On Bank Holidays the Cage was a rallying point for 'trippers,' for the park was open to the public and riddled with rights of way. On fine days they swarmed round the old building like bees, and though it was strictly forbidden (for trippers were not to be encouraged) no doubt Turner and his family compensated themselves for their lonely life by providing light refreshment for the visitors.

Vyne was practically self-supporting, for there was almost nothing pertaining to its upkeep which the estate employees could not do. A new entrance lodge had just been built of stone from the Vyne quarries, hewn, shaped and laid by the Vyne masons. The estate carpenters had fashioned the interior woodwork from timber grown, seasoned and sawn on the place, and Vyne painters and plasterers had completed the job. Hawkins, the clerk of the works, was a man of parts who could draw to scale and execute the plans for Lady Vayne's new rose garden and correct the perspective in Phyllis's sketches of the house. Jim Bowden, though not exactly a cabinet-maker, was certainly a skilled joiner and could be trusted to repair a Chippendale chair or a settee as well as any London expert. He could upholster too. Should Phyllis break a window whilst bowling yorkers to Piers in his bedroom (it was better than nothing whilst shut up after measles), then Gregory, the plumber and glazier, would come with his diamond-headed cutter and replace the pane. Mace, the electrician, in his great roaring and throbbing engine-room beside the mill-stream, generated the electricity which filled the house with brilliant light as well as supplying power for the laundry so that the maids no longer had to stand scrubbing and mangling the sheets and tablecloths by hand. Gardeners, gamekeepers, stablemen, road-menders, carters, farmworkers, here they all were assembled, each man proficient in his individual job, each a necessary part of the whole.

By the standards of a later generation their working hours were long and their wages low. They lived in cottages with no modern amenities yet came into daily contact with conditions of extreme comfort. They ministered to people whose lives must have appeared to them to be one continuous round of pleasure, whilst their own were lit only by occasional high days and holidays—the Wakes week, the flower show, the Christmas festival and perhaps once or twice in a lifetime the special glory of a coming of age or wedding anniversary. Yet it was more than doubtful if any of them envied their employer or wished him anything but good.

They were about halfway through the beef distribution, and the younger unmarried men were coming in now. Here was dark, sprightly Bob Wood with his flashing eyes and curly hair who worked in the blacksmith's shop and obviously had gipsy forbears. Bob was the crack batsman in the Vyne eleven and could always be counted upon to knock up some runs against the visiting teams who came on Saturday afternoons throughout the summer to play Vyne. One of these visiting teams with their offensive habit of calling "How's that?" much too often when Bob and Richard were batting was very unpopular with the younger Vaynes.

After him came Albert Whittle, Jock Whittle's delicate painter son. He had been very useful to Phyllis on one occasion. She also was supposed to be delicate and the doctor had prescribed raw beef sandwiches with milk at eleven. One morning, with Fräulein out of the way, Phyllis, seizing the plate of nauseous sandwiches, darted to the small bedroom at the foot of the tower which Albert and his mate were repainting and which was near the schoolroom. Opening the door just wide enough to insert her hand bearing the plate, in an assumed voice she invited Albert to eat the sandwiches. Then on the other side of the door she and Hilda listened, stifling their laughter whilst he obligingly did so, apparently with enjoyment.

Unfortunately, it had only been possible to do this

once, but mercifully the raw beef sandwiches were now things of the past.

Hilda, who liked helping people, was relieving her mother in the knotting up of the handkerchiefs, Lord Belgrave was talking to Lettice, Mr. Blunt had slipped away via the scullery, and the boys, followed by the two little girls, were roaming about the kitchen.

Apart from its immense size it had some curious and interesting features. Confronting the onlookers as they faced the door and the incoming men was a large pitch-pine erection about twelve feet square and eight feet high, a room within a room, its entrance screened by green baize curtains. This was Pérez's sanctum where he was wont to rest from his labours, sometimes sitting ruminating in solitary state, sometimes with Truelove occupying the other easy chair. Here Hilda and Phyllis would come in the morning to beg for chocolate, and he would always give them a whole packet of Menier which went so well with the milk and biscuits at eleven. Against one wall of the cubicle stood the pestle and mortar, the pestle reaching almost to the ceiling, the mortar as large as a church font. On the opposite wall hung the large pewter dish covers, handy for the serving hatch where the men servants came to fetch the dishes and carry them up the two flights of stairs to the dining-room. At the opposite end of the kitchen stood the huge range only newly installed, as its predecessor was found to be burning a ton of coal a day. A survival of former times was the large, semicircular, fluted lead sink which obviously had once held live fish before they appeared on the table.

The children could only guess at the various uses for the immense number of copper pans, moulds, salamanders and bains-marie which covered the shelves, and marvel at the great array of cook's knives carefully graded and laid out on the long tables. It never occurred to any of them to speculate as to the amount of time and trouble entailed in keeping all these implements as well as the vast

 kitchen itself in perfect condition. That it should always look as now, the floor clean and freshly sanded, the tables scrubbed white and the kettles and pans shining like mirrors, they took for granted. Each kitchen maid wore a replica of Pérez's white cap, a recent innovation which Lady Vayne did not much care for, preferring the more feminine style worn by the housemaids, but the chef had his way. Moody and temperamental, one could never know when his smiles would be replaced by frowns.

Sometimes Hilda and Phyllis passing the kitchen windows on their way to feed their rabbits would hear sounds of shrill altercation mingling with Pérez's rich baritone. If sufficiently interested to stop and peer over the ground glass of the lower panes, Pérez could be seen, a commanding figure in his high cook's cap, white tunic and apron and scarlet leather top-boots which he always wore when at work. But almost at once, perhaps aware of an audience, when the din to which he was largely contribut-

ing was at its height he would let fall a dignified "Assez
—assez!" and produce an instantaneous hush. Probably,
despite his moods and Madame Pérez in the background,
a good deal of fun as well as hard work went on in the
kitchen.

Poor Pérez, so much of his best work seemed to go

Pérez and his maids

unregarded. There were not enough gourmets at Vyne to
appreciate him. Though Sir Thomas, despite austerity,
very decidedly preferred good cooking to bad, he was just
as pleased with a grilled herring as a sole au vin blanc. The
timbales de bœuf, the pâtés de lièvre, the truffled galan-
tines, concocted with so much care and sent up with such
a desire to please, how often they came down untouched!
The boys did their best, but the most artistic efforts were
wasted on them, preferring as they did the huge spec-
tacular boar's head with its pistachio nut tusks which

always appeared on the sideboard at Christmas. "*Miladi*," he once complained tearfully to Lady Vayne when nothing but cold meat was served at luncheon and she demanded an explanation, "*Toute cette belle viande froide! Personne la mange! Il faut bien qu'on la mange!*" And of course he was perfectly right.

Piers was questioning Rose, the head kitchen maid, as to what they were having for dinner, and because Piers undoubtedly had 'a way with him' she had no objection to replying at length.

"You kids needn't listen," he said to Phyllis and Alethea, who were hovering round. "You belong in the schoolroom with Fräulein. Phyllis, I'm seriously considering whether you ought to come down to dinner tomorrow." His mouth was twitching at the corners and his eyes glinting with mischief for Piers was certainly a born tease and found in Phyllis an ideal subject for his wit. Knowing perfectly where to find the joints in her armour, he would at a well-chosen moment start to bait her, delighting in the furious but rather inarticulate response which he never failed to evoke. Although very good-natured, the idea that he might be overdoing it and causing real distress never seemed to occur to him, and Lady Vayne, who thought Phyllis should learn to take a joke and not mind being laughed at, did nothing to stop him. She was, anyhow, not an impartial judge, as in her eyes her sons could do no wrong. However, to-night, strange to say, even Phyllis perceived Piers's intention and refused to rise to the fly. Piers could be very amusing in a slightly ribald way. This kind of fooling was rather prevalent at Christmas, Mr. Blunt being a past-master at it. Fräulein sometimes looked down her nose at his jokes and his oft repeated snatch of song: "My sister Ann had a leg like a man." He also liked teasing Phyllis. Sometimes in London when high hopes of the pantomime had been aroused, he would terrify her with proposals of some other most unwelcome alternative.

"We're going to Exeter Hall," he would announce, and whether this place really existed or he had invented it she never discovered. But, anyhow, at Exeter Hall it seemed people gathered in order to sing hymns and say prayers with a dreadful person presiding who, without warning, would single out some luckless member of the audience (or congregation) and ask them questions out of scripture.

"He's sure to ask you, Phyllis, so mind you're well up in Bible history or he'll be annoyed. Then when question time is over there'll be more prayers and hymn singing. Very pleasant and elevating. I'm sure you'll enjoy it."

Phyllis's face would grow longer and longer till her mother took pity on her. "It's all right, darling. We're going to Drury Lane to see Dan Leno in 'Mother Goose.'"

Sometimes there was hoaxing of a different kind. A disreputable-looking hawker who arrived with some live ducks for sale, and sold Sir Thomas a pair of his own pin-tail, turned out to be Mr. Blunt. Another time he was an American come to England to study country house life, talking about 'vaises' meaning vases, and 'closets' meaning cupboards, saying 'pleased to meet you, Marquis' to Lord Belgrave, who happened to be staying; and the show was only given away by Sir Thomas (who, of course was in the know) guffawing with laughter when the American said: "Ah'm tauld there's nuthin in this harse later than Stephen."

When the last name had been read out, the last joint

tied up and the shepherd's apron was no longer immaculate, the family left the kitchen to return upstairs, repassing as they did so the double rank of figures still lining the long passage, who, as they scurried past, gave them as a final valediction three loud and ringing cheers.

"That," said Sir Thomas to Lord Belgrave as they mounted the pantry stairs, "is the most artificial part of the whole proceedings."

Phyllis wished her father would not say things like that even if he believed them, which she doubted. Wasn't it only natural that they should feel sufficient good will towards a kind employer to wish to cheer him and his family on Christmas Eve? But it was all part of the strange inhibition from which he suffered, which also prevented him from uttering a single word of endearment to any of his family, though his love was plainly visible for all to see.

It was the same with his home.

Sometimes in the summer acquaintances visiting a neighbouring spa would risk the breakdown of their none too reliable motor cars on the steep hills to see this place famed for its exceptional and haunting beauty. Brought into being, guarded, embellished, tended and cherished for centuries solely by one otherwise rather humdrum family, it constituted their chief claim to distinction, and in creating and preserving it they might be said to have justified their existence. Eagerly the visitors followed Lady Vayne on a tour of the house, listening to her account of its history whilst she displayed everything with loving pride. And in the background Sir Thomas would be doing his best to discount everything his wife said. Of the wood carvings in the saloon, after she had drawn attention to the various enchanting motifs

—the lace handkerchief, the musical instruments, the delicate bird's claws, the artist's palette and brushes, he would say: "Obviously the work of Gibbons's pupils." Of the panelling in the Long Gallery: "You see, this is only sham oak, not the real thing." Of the state bed in which James II had slept when Duke of York: "Almost every house of this sort has something of the kind, and anyhow it's been spoilt by the curtains being relined." Or, if it was not the house, it was the climate, or the pollution of the atmosphere from the nearby industrial town, or the stunted growth of the trees on the Cage hill, which at such an altitude could hardly be expected to soar luxuriantly, till his children could willingly have turned and rent him. Phyllis felt instinctively it was due to a kind of perverse pride: "I love my home and am proud of it, but no one shall ever hear me say so," was her best guess as to what he must really feel.

They had no sooner regained the first floor than the sound of the dressing-gong booming through the house gave the signal for the grown-ups to disperse to their rooms and for the little girls, including Hilda, to say goodnight. It was characteristic of the times that Hilda, only about a year younger than Piers, was still condemned to schoolroom supper whilst he, because of his superior sex, had for several years now eaten all his meals in the dining-room.

Phyllis and Alethea accompanied Aunt Lucy to her room, which was off the central stretch of the first floor corridor. Here it broadened into a gallery along which stood marquetry, lacquer and walnut cabinets and high-backed chairs; and on the walls were family portraits and pictures of the house in its first youth.

Every window embrasure held pots of flowers. The windows themselves were curtainless but covered by

The Tudor window in the gatehouse

blinds hanging in fringed festoons, every one of which had been made by Mrs. Campbell with the help of her machine and the spinster sister of one of the gardeners. Each blind had to be sewn with about a gross of brass rings through which the tapes were passed which held the material in its gathered loops, and poor Mrs. Campbell often bewailed the wearisome work which she nevertheless accomplished so faithfully and well.

Drawing aside one of these blinds, Phyllis looked out into the dark courtyard. The window in the gate-house, with its small, diamond-shaped panes which looked on to the inner court and behind which John, the hall-porter, slept, was lit and showed a white, even expanse of newly fallen snow completely covering the flags of the courtyard.

That was as it should be—a white Christmas. When the curtain went up at the given moment it would be on the perfect Christmas scene. Phyllis knew the exact moment when the curtain would rise—not when she first woke in the morning and felt for the bulges in the stocking at the foot of her bed. It was a little later when the strains of 'Christians, awake' sung by the carol singers in the courtyard below penetrated to her bedroom.

The reception of these carol singers was the only part of the Christmas festivities which seemed to be not quite perfect. They were not the ordinary waits out to receive alms, but members of the unusually well-trained choir from the village church, whose organist and choir-master happened to be a skilled musician. In the still air of early morning from the enclosed courtyard their voices soared sweet and true and clear:

> *The praises of redeeming love they sang,*
> *And Heaven's whole orb with Alleluias rang.*

Yet, strangely enough, no one seemed to appreciate their performance nor the fact that they had climbed the two miles of continuously rising ground from the park gates in the frost and snow of winter to sing to the occupants of the great house. What was more, having sung, they would then have to tramp back again.

Phyllis felt rather ashamed that up till now she had never bothered to find out when or where they were given refreshment. It was not after their singing, for she had seen them walking away from the seemingly still sleeping house. No doubt Truelove gave them breakfast on arrival: some of them were friends of his—Mr. Swan the schoolmaster and Miss Bennet from the post office—and some would be coming as guests to the Servants' Ball on New Year's Eve, which formed the climax of the Christmas festivities. But it was rather strange, she now thought for the first time, she could not recall either of her parents ever mentioning them. For they were the overture to the Christmas drama!

She might, if she had been older, have remembered it is the fate of most overtures to be disregarded.

Alethea wanted to stay with her mother whilst she dressed for dinner, but Aunt Lucy would not allow this.

"You've had a long journey and you must get to bed early," she said. "Besides, it's time for your supper, and mind, you two, you're not to wake up in the middle of the night and start looking at your stockings." She was sitting in an armchair by the fire, taking off her boots, and after saying this she suddenly threw herself back in her chair, waved her legs in the air and cried: "Hurrah! Christmas Day to-morrow."

Aunt Lucy, like her brother William, sometimes gave expression to feelings of joy in very childlike ways, a characteristic which Phyllis's mother also shared and which not even the powerful brake of Vayne reserve could altogether curb. Alethea echoed her mother's exuberance, but the equally if not more joyous-hearted Phyllis only smiled indulgently. No one knew better than she how one felt on Christmas Eve, but the Vaynes were

strange people. They might display anger but not joy—
their joy, it seemed, was too intimate a thing to be shown
to anyone—only, perhaps, to God.

They said goodnight and proceeded to disregard the
instructions of mother and aunt to go straight to supper
and then to bed by going instead to the Long Gallery.

"Fräulein won't mind our being a bit late to-night,"
said Phyllis, and led Alethea up another side staircase to
the top corridor, this time along the front of the house, so
that they entered the gallery by the door at the opposite
end to the stage.

The room was now in complete darkness, but Phyllis
groped for the switch by the door and the great length of
the gallery leapt into view.

The Christmas tree was fully decorated, and they
stopped first to inspect this before strolling on to the
stage. It was not forbidden to look at the tree before
Christmas Day, but no one might go into that part of the
gallery behind the stage where all the presents were laid
out on the billiard table.

Truelove had as usual made a thoroughly good job of
the tree. The shape was now perfect, thanks to the additional branches, which no one, without being told, could
possibly have detected. There were rainbow-coloured,
iridescent glass balls hanging singly and in garlands,
showers of sparkling tinsel, spun glass humming birds,
bells and stars, trumpets and violins, small toy crocodiles
and golliwogs, a figure of Father Christmas on the top-
most branch and, of course, innumerable candles.

Having examined the tree at length, they turned their attention to the stage. Phyllis switched on the footlights and the woodland scene was revealed in all its glory.

When they started rehearsals on Boxing Day, it would be under difficulties. On this day the pheasants were shot for the second time and neither the men nor the boys would be at rehearsal. They would all be home for lunch though, and all told one hundred persons would sit down to their mid-day meal at Vyne.

For the first rehearsal, therefore, Mr. Blunt, who did not shoot, would have only the ladies and little girls at his disposal.

Phyllis did not always enjoy rehearsals. She had no difficulty in memorising her part; what was so difficult was the playing of it. She sometimes wondered why success had seemed to come so easily, almost effortlessly, a year or two ago—no one had yet enlightened her and she was too young to find the answer for herself. The answer, of course, was to be found in that all too common failing—that terrible selfconsciousness growing with the years which must inevitably be destructive of all natural grace. A little older, the player might acquire enough artifice to conceal it—a little younger, there was nothing to conceal.

Quite rightly Mr. Blunt was not easily satisfied. Sometimes, but not often, he would say, "Charming, Babbles, charming" (he called her this, her mother's name for her, when he was pleased), but more often he would cover his face with his hands and groan.

Singing, too, was an ordeal, and the highest praise she had won was from her father, who had said: "Phyllis can always sing in tune."

Alethea, on the other hand, was not only a born actress but possessed a charming little singing voice which had already received some training. It hardly seemed fair, thought Phyllis a little ruefully, though not resentfully, that in addition to her looks Alethea should be so talented.

Hilda generally played a character part, and this year she was to double the roles of gipsy soothsayer and a maid in the highwayman piece which followed. Mr. Blunt took the part of Phyllis's wicked guardian. He was really an ideal producer, giving the closest attention to detail. In last year's production Harry had to call attention to some distant sound off-stage by saying "Hark!"

"You can't say that, it's too much like 'Bark,'" objected Mr. Blunt.

"Hush, then," suggested Harry.

"No, that's like ghost."

"Listen" was at last agreed upon.

Somebody else had to lie down on a sofa and go to sleep.

"What are the soles of your shoes like?" he asked. "You can't put up a great pair of white soles."

The children were always being exhorted to bear in mind that their voices had to carry the whole length of the room. "Speak up! Speak up and don't say your lines to the backcloth," was Mr. Blunt's continual cry.

In spite of everything, though, rehearsing was rather fun, perhaps for the very reason that the best was expected from everyone.

Behind the stage the gallery broadened out considerably and was used as a Green Room, all the stage properties being laid out on the billiard table. Mr. Blunt made everybody up in his bedroom, which was close at hand, the end room of the bachelors' passage which ran parallel with the Long Gallery and looked on to the inner court-yard. It was fun watching him do it.

"Give me beetling eyebrows," said Piers when he was being made up as the poor but honest peasant. "I want beetling eyebrows like yours."

Oh, the delicious, thrilling smell of greasepaint and rouge and all that they stood for! Waiting on the set but darkened stage, dressed in fascinating transforming gar-ments, peeping through a slit in the lowered curtain at the rows of faces in the audience, seeing a like transforma-tion in all one's familiar companions, Richard a cavalier with a large curly hat. Mama in a towering white wig and hooped skirts, Hilda a witch in a sugar-loaf hat, and Mr. Blunt a villainous highwayman in a mask!

Three evenings were devoted to the theatricals. The first, the dress rehearsal, which everybody in the house attended, usually went off without a hitch. On the second the élite of the county and magnates from the industrial town came with their families, a small charge being made for admission, the proceeds going to the local infirmary. The final performance was attended by the tenants, work-people and villagers. Truelove acted as prompter, but it was rare for anyone to require his services—except, oddly enough, Mr. Blunt.

It might here be questioned whether even at the start of the century people were willing to put up with this kind of thing even at Christmas and in a play performed chiefly by children. But they were. A very small section of the audience might not be altogether sorry when the entertainment drew to its triumphant close, but they remained a tiny minority; and when it is remembered that at two out of three of the performances there were always some members of the audience who could neither read nor write, that there was no competition from cinemas or wireless, that the nearest professional entertainment was fifteen miles distant and that most people were still dependent on horse-drawn vehicles and bicycles, the undoubted success of the Vyne theatricals seems less surprising.

After walking about on the stage for some time admiring the woodland scene and exchanging opinions about their parts, Phyllis and Alethea finally left the gallery by the door giving on to the grand staircase.

Here they met Mr. Blunt coming up very late to dress for dinner. "If you don't all know your parts perfectly by Boxing Day I'll kiss the lot of you," he said threateningly as he passed them.

"Oh, we can't risk that, we'll know them all right," Alethea called after him, and Phyllis wondered admiringly how she had learnt to say things like that already.

Once through the door at the head of the stairs, the appearance of the corridor changed considerably, drugget instead of Persian runners on the floor, only the throwouts of the pictures on the plain, unwainscoted walls, and plain calico blinds at the windows.

In the schoolroom Fräulein and Hilda were waiting with supper on the table and Hilda was inclined to be a little resentful.

"Where *have* you been, Phyllis? I know Aunt Lucy

wanted Alethea to go to bed early to-night, and we've been waiting ages for you!"

Alethea was gentle and placating, Phyllis less so. Fräulein, still indulgently forbearing, led them to the table and called on Phyllis to say grace.

Mike was not present, but Lady, the big mastiff, lay in her usual place in front of the fire. She was the last of her

Lady

breed, the famous breed of Vyne mastiffs, of which there was documentary proof that a pair had been sent along with other gifts by James I to the King of Spain. A copy of Velasquez's picture "Las Meninas" hung on the grand staircase, and certainly the dog in the picture bore a great resemblance to Lady and might well have been a descendant of the famous pair. People said what a pity it was to let the breed die out, but Sir Thomas was too great a lover of dogs to keep a pack of useless animals fretting their hearts out behind bars and only let out for exercise; for even at Vyne one huge dog in the house was enough: and so Lady was the last of her breed.

The children were rather silent at supper, Alethea a

little weary, Hilda and Phyllis thinking of to-morrow night when they would not be sitting up here with Fräulein but dressed in their best, forming part of the festive gathering downstairs.

There would be additional guests in the persons of Canon and Mrs. Waldegrave and Mr. Hunt, the curate.

Canon Waldegrave was a tall, beautiful old man with a Grecian profile and a white beard. When seated meditatively under the east window in the chancel whilst Mr. Hunt occupied the pulpit (it was his custom to leave his curate to preach the sermon almost every Sunday) he was the embodiment of Phyllis's idea of an ancient Druid, though in reality much more like a Greek philosopher. Mrs. Waldegrave was a little scrap of a woman always dressed in black with a large lace cap.

The place of assembly before meals was the library— the least beautiful of the principal rooms—and the books lining its walls were with one exception of small value. Lady Vayne maintained that, when shown this one exception, the lady librarian of Chatsworth had actually betrayed signs of envy! The one ewe lamb, as Lady Vayne called it, was nothing less than the earliest known edition of the Sarum Missal, printed for Caxton in Paris in 1487—but how and when this unique volume had been acquired the family history did not reveal.

When everybody had assembled in the library and Truelove had announced dinner, they would process into the dining-room, Sir Thomas taking in Mrs. Waldegrave, and Lady Vayne bringing up the rear with the Canon. Probably Cousin Amy would be allotted to Mr. Hunt. The boys and girls would bunch in together at the last. Through the little tapestried anteroom they would pass into the big Georgian dining-room. The long table extending almost the entire length of the room would glitter and sparkle with the lights reflected in the silver and the white of the cloth and from the walls the family portraits would smile benignly on the company. On one of the four gilt side-tables would stand the wonderful rose-water dish and ewer, silver and parcel-gilt with the Vayne

 arms embossed in coloured enamels—made in the reign of Bloody Mary. (Truelove had discovered this treasure, its existence apparently unknown, in the depths of a plate chest.)

The footmen would be wearing their knee-breeches —so much Sir Thomas had had to concede for special occasions—but they were of the plainest, most unobtrusive black, nothing like the gorgeous confections Phyllis had caught sight of in certain grand houses in London. Uncle William's and Lord Belgrave's valets would be helping to wait, for the company would number about thirty.

They would begin with grace said by the Canon and then the meal would proceed eaten off silver plates, not so pleasant as the china service because scratchy under the knife and fork, but welcome because they were part of the Christmas ritual. The candle shades in the tall candelabras had little garlands of silver spangles and there would be crackers laid amongst the flower decorations.

First there would be soup of the clearest consistency imaginable, and then some kind of fish which melted in the mouth. Then an entrée, perhaps a vol au vent or small mutton cutlets, and then roast turkey or pheasant. Then a wonderful sweet into which Pérez had put all his artistry: perhaps baskets of nougat with ribbons of spun sugar containing a creamy ice, and muscat grapes coated in sugar and crystallised quarters of orange and tiny pastry cakes.

The last course, the savoury, was never handed to the little girls. Without any instruction in the matter Truelove had made this decision, and nobody questioned it. On the other hand, he always allowed them a little champagne. Dessert was almost the nicest part of the meal, and the scent of tangerine oranges would all her life be associated in Phyllis's mind with Christmas dinner at Vyne.

With dessert came the crackers, always a trial to Sir Thomas, for whom the sight of grown men and women in paper caps was anathema.

When the last cracker had been pulled, the mottoes read, the puzzles examined and the jewellery and toys appropriated, Lady Vayne would somehow down the great length of the table manage to catch Mrs. Waldegrave's eye and the ladies would leave the dining-room, passing out by a door opposite to that by which they had entered, into another tapestried anteroom containing Stuart relics. This, like its fellow flanking the dining-room, was pure Jacobean. A painted plaster frieze in high relief contained medallions depicting the life of the stag, and over the chimney-piece the house, as it was in the seventeenth century, was sandwiched between two groups of stags standing one upon the other and almost as large as the house. Below this again two figures symbolising peace and plenty with the Stuart coat of arms between them. A glass case held the precious relics, Charles I's embroidered gloves and his agate-hilted dagger. Sometimes poring over the contents of this case, fascinated by the thought that Charles's hands had grasped that dagger, worn those long-fingered gloves, Phyllis would marvel that the same term could apply to these richly embroidered, gold-laced works of art and the

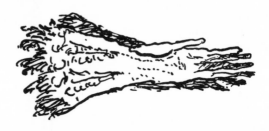

machine-made, strictly utilitarian articles she wore on her own little chapped hands. A portrait of the Martyr King in Puritan dress painted just before his execution, his death warrant in his hand, hung beside the fireplace. But best of all were the six Chippendale chairs, their backs carved with the entwined scrolls C.R., their seats covered with the embroidered cloth which had been Charles's cloak and for which these peerless chairs had been made. Without pausing, the procession of ladies would pass through this Jacobean anteroom, which was known as the Stag parlour, into the Elizabethan drawing-room.

Everyone is only too familiar with the cliché, "One seemed on entering to step back into the past." But no words could be more adequate to describe the impression made by this room.

Although, or perhaps because, it was only used on special occasions, it possessed a more individual atmosphere than any other room at Vyne. Even the most insensitive were touched by it. It seemed to breathe peace; to murmur of happiness, a happiness of lives spent in love and charity; and leisure which had not been abused and humility whose pride was service.

The walls were oak-panelled to within three feet of the ceiling in an elaborate pattern of pillars with interlacing arches inlaid in places with satinwood. Above this a deep plaster frieze with masks and scallop shells, gilded and painted and in high relief. In this Elizabethan setting stood furniture—acquired by successive generations—ranging in period from the sixteenth to the late eighteenth century and the result was a complete harmony. Gilt tables with cabriole legs stood beside high-backed carved Stuart chairs; above them hung portraits of the same period and gilt girandoles by Chippen-  dale surmounted by birds. Chippendale settees were set beside Jacobean elbow chairs. In the huge Tudor chimney-piece, almost a counterpart of the one in the Long Gallery, stood a cut steel Adam grate, and the whorls and bosses of the ceiling were repeated in the close pattern of the carpet. But the chief feature of the room was the wide bay, its three long windows filled with sixteenth-century heraldic glass which in the daytime

Smiling her Mona Lisa smile

glowed and glimmered in squares and lozenges of emerald, ruby, sapphire and topaz like the contents of a giantess's jewel case. In the central window was set a miniature portrait of the Elizabethan Sir Piers in beard and ruff. Guarding the entrance to these splendours like tall twin sentinels, on Chippendale brackets each side of the bay stood blanc de Chine figures of the goddess Kuan Yin, smiling her Mona Lisa smile.

Seated at schoolroom supper Phyllis pictured in her mind's eye exactly how it would be to-morrow night.

Grandmamma, who did not come in to dinner, would be waiting for them on the settee by the fire in her rose-coloured silk dress.

Phyllis was never quite at her ease with her grandmother. Perhaps it was because she was very easily moved to tears and seemed to feel things so intensely.

Lady Vayne might be recounting how someone, perhaps Richard, had been suffering from one of the usual complaints of youth, measles or chicken-pox, which was now, however, happily over. Grandmamma would exclaim in broken accents: "Poor boy, poor boy," and dissolve in tears. Or perhaps Phyllis, who was growing fast, was looking a little tired. "That child's terribly pale," she would say in tragic tones. One never knew who would be the next object of her concern. Old age, which makes so many people seemingly indifferent to events, seemed to have increased her capacity for feeling.

Aunt Lucy knew best how to handle her. To-morrow evening there would be a short interlude whilst they all gathered round her and coffee was being served. A few tenderly bantering remarks would have to be made by Aunt Lucy, one or two humorous anecdotes retailed by Cousin Amy, before they could all settle down, Mrs. Waldegrave, Lady Vayne and Aunt Lucy beside the settee, another and far larger group round the card table, of which Fräulein would be the centre of interest, for this was her time for telling the cards.

Aunt Sybil, Sir Thomas's sister, had a great belief in Fräulein's psychic powers. She and Cousin Amy would be the first to have their fortunes told, then Lettice and Hilda, lastly Alethea and Phyllis.

The little girls were not much interested as yet, except in the part where one was told about getting one's wish, and that was thrilling. There was always a dark woman making a nuisance of herself and a dark man in trouble or ill. A fair man was in love with a fair woman and a lot of people at the house, most of which one knew already. Probably the queen of diamonds, which was Lettice, and the king of diamonds would come out next each other, and Aunt Sybil would exclaim how uncanny the cards were, for everyone knew Captain Tarporley to be a serious admirer of Lettice's.

By the time the cards were told the men would emerge from the dining-room. Sir Thomas never kept them long, even though he would be sure to want to talk to Lord Belgrave about the bill for National Service he hoped to bring before Parliament and which Lord Belgrave was to sponsor in the Lords. Sir Thomas was the sitting member for one of the County Divisions, having been more fortunate than his brother-in-law, who had lost his seat in the recent Liberal landslide. Phyllis could well remember the day when the bad news had arrived.

They had just started out for a drive, and meeting the telegraph boy on his way up to the house Lady Vayne stopped the carriage and with eager, trembling fingers tore open the telegram. "Withinshaw returned," she read out in accents of despair, and Phyllis, who was unfamiliar with political phraseology, could only guess that Uncle William had not got in.

He had represented a rather red industrial town, whereas Sir Thomas's constituency was mainly rural, and in addition in those parts the name Vayne of Vyne would secure the votes of all but the reddest radicals.

With the appearance of the men there would be a general exodus to the hall. Then a round game would be started, perhaps Racing Demon, perhaps Up Jenkins, or possibly Charades. Mr. Hunt would be included but not the Canon or his wife. Lord Belgrave would probably play billiards with Uncle Andrew on the miniature table. Mr. Blunt and Uncle William each in their own way would be the moving spirits of the round game. In one called Impertinent Questions, Piers and Mr. Blunt would sometimes overstep the mark and cause Fräulein to look down her pointed nose. Lady Vayne never took part in the games. She would be seated quietly talking to the Canon on the sofa or simply looking on. Sometimes she suffered from a feeling of irritation of the skin, and if seated by Phyllis would perhaps whisper to her in an interval of the game. Then Phyllis, unobtrusively but quite unconcernedly and without anyone seeming to notice or care, would pass her short finger-nails to and fro over her mother's bare shoulders till the irritation was allayed or it was time to resume the game. She often ministered to her mother in this way and was rather proud to be the one always chosen to do so. The entrance of the servants with the tray of drinks was the signal that the evening was nearly at an end and very shortly after Mrs. Waldegrave would make a move and the first perfect day would be over.

Phyllis had to rouse herself from her happy reverie to attend to Alethea, who was talking about Christmas presents. Would it be best to keep their own particular gifts for the tree or give them beforehand?

"We always give ours to Papa and Mama before breakfast," said Hilda. "And the ones for each other after church. There's just time before luncheon."

By mutual agreement the cousins never gave each other presents; the state of their finances would not have allowed it.

"Are you going to the wishing well these holidays, Hilda?" asked Alethea.

A pleased, reminiscent look came into her cousin's eyes.

A year or two ago before Fräulein's reign she had gone every day of the holidays to the wishing well to wish for the removal of an unpleasant governess. The wish had been granted soon after.

Wishing Well Wood was the loveliest in the park. In the late spring the high banks on either side of the drive which ran through it were clothed in bluebells—in the autumn with bracken. A little rushing stream ran beside the drive, and sometimes on the boulders at its edge there was a thick white froth which looked so exactly like icecream that Phyllis had once, to Fräulein's disgust, tasted it. But it tasted of nothing. The wishing well was in a little fern-fringed stone basin beside the drive. Three times one drank from the cold, delicious water and wished, then threw the last handful over the left shoulder. Near the wishing well was the turning to the quarry, a wild, uncanny place of towering stone cliffs, tawny-yellow, almost rose-coloured in places, the stone from which the south front of Vyne had been built. This quarry was still worked, and Hilda had once found a note lying on a shelf of stone: "Come and bring your tools to the south front." Evidently some minor repair in the masonry was needed.

The last drive of the pheasant shoot was in this wood, the guns being stationed along the drive, and the birds driven from the high ground above came over at such a height that even the best shots often missed.

Fräulein remarked that Alethea was looking tired, and Alethea admitted she was a little and agreed to go to bed directly they had finished eating. Phyllis for her own reasons made no objection, and accordingly they bade goodnight to Fräulein and Hilda and parted from each other at the door of the schoolroom.

On entering her room, Phyllis found Lettice just emerging from her own to go down to dinner.

Lettice's room, access to which could only be gained through Phyllis's, was in that angle of the house against which at certain seasons of the year the south-west gales beat and battered with greatest fury.

Sometimes, Lettice said, she thought the walls would collapse and go crashing into the Italian garden forty feet below. But in summer she slept peacefully to the sound of the splashing fountain.

She was looking radiant to-night in a dress of green and

[71]

silver tissue. Having just been put on an allowance, she was able to indulge her individual taste. She favoured the soft greens and mauves of the iris, and where other girls wore high stiff collars in the daytime she preferred low-necked blouses.

Phyllis glanced approvingly at her sister as she paused to give one more look at herself in Phyllis's long, narrow mirror.

"I do like that dress, Lettice."

"Yes, it's not bad, is it?"

"What will you wear to-morrow night?"

"Oh, I don't know, my green tulle I expect."

"I do think Captain Tarporley's nice, don't you?"

"Yes, quite." Lettice touched the little curls under her pompadour.

It was a great concession Captain Tarporley's being allowed to play the 'jeune premier' to Lettice's 'ingénue' instead of it being as usual given to Harry. Any young man who came to the house was immediately a suspect to Sir Thomas, who, whilst taking pride in her powers of attraction, dreaded the loss of his eldest daughter's companionship through marriage.

But it was quite evidently a loss he would have to face sooner or later.

Lettice sometimes treated her young sister as a confidante. She had once asked Phyllis what one had better do supposing one liked somebody very much but wasn't quite sure if one wanted to marry him. Phyllis thought for a little then gave her considered opinion.

It would be best to tell him she wasn't sure, but if he liked to wait and nobody else came along she liked better Lettice might take him.

But Lettice said no. It wasn't fair to keep a man dangling in case no one better turned up. One simply could not do such things—and Phyllis felt rather ashamed of what had seemed to her a very sensible solution.

The gong sounding whilst Lettice was having her final look at herself, the sisters bade each other goodnight and Lettice vanished through the door to the grand staircase.

Phyllis should by rights have started undressing, but she could hear Louisa still tidying up in the next room, and seizing her opportunity turned and ran down the passage in the opposite direction.

The great entrance hall at Vyne stood on a level of its own, above the cloisters but below the first floor; a short flight of stairs at either end connecting it with the passage which ran round the other three sides of the courtyard. Above the hall lay the Long Gallery, below it the dark, vaulted passage between the kitchen and the servants' hall.

To enter the hall from outside one mounted a double flight of stone steps in the inner courtyard. Inside, to right and left of the central doorway, other doors gave access to the rest of the house; and dividing this passage-way from the main portion of the room stood a row of towering Corinthian pillars, for the hall was both large and lofty. Great pieces of Mortlake tapestry covered three of the walls, depicting · the story of Hero and Leander in the glowing umbers, blues and crimsons of the seventeenth century: the lovers standing with clasped hands before a columned building, a cupid with bent bow hovering over their heads, Hero peeping through her doorway at Leander prone in the swirling waters, which seemed threatening to flood the house, Hero alone upon the shore, hands raised to heaven, her draperies fluttering in the breeze. Over the chimney-piece hung a three-quarter length portrait of the ubiquitous Elizabethan Sir Piers, one long-fingered hand resting on his gold-embossed sword, the hilt of which was still preserved among the family relics.

In the words of a well-worn cliché—the owner of those impassive features might have been meditating on the vanity of human affairs: of what account were man's ambitions, his pains and pleasures, hopes and fears, viewed against the background of eternity, etc.? Without doubt those impassive features had, through the centuries, witnessed countless scenes both grave and gay in this same room. Here his descendants and their servants had rendered daily homage to Almighty God, the men filing in at one door, the women at another, and the head of the house from a central position, surrounded by his family, had read the prayers. Only in the last year or so had this practice been discontinued. It was too patriarchal, pompous and, anyhow, hard luck on the servants, said Sir Thomas, neglecting to add that he found it personally embarrassing.

At the same time, services in the chapel, which of course ante-dated family prayers in the hall, had also been dropped. Lady Vayne, a little troubled about this, was nevertheless consoled by the fact that the chapel which adjoined the servants' hall with the drawing-room above it, had not been consecrated. In the old days when there had been a resident chaplain, and everyone on the property had attended as a matter of course, it was worth the trouble of training the maidservants to sing in the choir. But now, after morning service in the parish church, evensong in the chapel was more than could be expected of anybody. Alas, alas! The chapel had gradually become a storing place for surplus furniture, chairs and rout seats for dances and Fräulein's bicycle, whilst the hall was given up to relaxation, music, dancing and games. It made a perfect ballroom, and on New Year's Eve was cleared of all its furniture and the oak floorboards carefully polished for that great event to which both servants and children looked forward with such eagerness—the Servants' Ball.

As was fitting for such an occasion, a tray of buttonholes made the round of the bedrooms before dinner, single flowers for the gentlemen, larger sprays for the ladies. Dinner was curtailed and hurried over and the members of the house party, after donning their white kid gloves, waited patiently in the drawing-room till summoned to the hall. Meanwhile the band arrived and took up its position, with much tuning of instruments, on the raised platform at one end of the ballroom. One of the side doors would open and Truelove, with Mrs. Campbell on his arm, emerge, followed in pairs by the other servants in strict order of precedence. Strangely enough, their guests came last, for each servant was allowed to invite one friend; and thus, with the heads of the outdoor staff and their wives and the members of the house party, a sufficient company was formed to fill the large room.

Here it might be noted that the Servants' Balls at Vyne differed from some which were held in other great houses in that they took place above stairs not below; and that everybody from highest to lowest was expected to attend.

When all were assembled, the party in the drawing-room entered and the band burst into the strains of the opening dance.

Invariably Lady Vayne opened the ball; invariably also the opening dance, the tune and the assignment of partners were the same each year. There was, however, one notable

Haste to the wedding

absentee. Truelove, a devout Plymouth Brother, disapproved of dancing, and when the ceremony of leading in Mrs. Campbell was complete, he would retire from the scene. In his absence, therefore, Lady Vayne was partnered by Ruggles, the coachman, Sir Thomas with Mrs. Campbell, Lettice, Hilda and Phyllis with the bailiff, head gardener and the clerk of the works; Richard with the bailiff's wife. Piers took Pont for his partner, and the others danced with whom they pleased.

A little aigrette with a diamond star in her hair, a malmaison in her corsage, her train sweeping after her, down the double line of dancers sailed Lady Vayne with the fat Ruggles, very conscious of his importance as master of ceremonies, bounding light as a feather by her side, in perfect time to the music. Up the middle and down again, hands round with the next couple, then up the middle again, followed, this time, by Mrs. Campbell with Sir Thomas wearing his embarrassed schoolboy air.

Rumpty *tump*tity, tumptity, tumpty tum went the reiterated rhythm of 'Haste to the Wedding' over and over again. Although they did it every year, nobody except Ruggles, Mrs. Campbell and Lady Vayne seemed to understand the procedure of the dance, and long before the band had had enough, there was complete confusion. After this time-honoured beginning people relaxed a little. The house party were expected to keep to their end of the room between dances. At the other end sat the wives of the head employees, usually rather soberly garbed in very high-collared dresses. There was Mrs. Ruggles of the stables, Mrs. Archer of the gardens, Mrs. Ardern of the kennels, Mrs. Hawkins, wife of the head carpenter or clerk of the works, and highest-ranking Mrs. Cotton of the Home Farm. Although some of them were only in the thirties and Mrs. Cotton had considerable claims to beauty, they did not much concern themselves with fashion and Mrs. Archer, a red-haired woman of very rugged appearance, habitually wore a man's black billycock banded with light blue ribbon whenever she took the air. As they rarely joined in the dancing they were all the better able to observe every detail of the scene —whether her Ladyship and Miss Lettice were wearing new dresses or ones they had seen before, whether Miss Pont had made a success of her own dress or not, and how often Lord Belgrave's valet (he was known to be a married man) danced with the prettiest of the laundry maids.

At last year's ball a distinct sensation had been caused by one young lady who came in a very low-cut evening frock, which was quite unprecedented. Her appearance was, in fact, so exquisite, with her tall elegant figure and graceful queenly bearing, that it seemed almost a condescension on her part to have come. Mr. Blunt of course said he should ask her to dance and bring her to sit with the house party. Harry took him seriously and said he should ask her first, and Piers too was much intrigued. What was more, the lady had brought with her a brother as good-looking as herself, and he too was in faultless evening dress, perfectly cut tail-coat and white waistcoat.

Who was responsible for introducing this pair of swans among the more homely geese was never divulged. Truelove was suspected by some, for though he disapproved of dancing, he oddly enough had no objection to asking his friends to the ball. One thing, however, was certain—he would not allow it to occur again. They had committed a solecism in coming to the ball dressed exactly as the gentry. It was as bad as if Mr. Blunt had appeared in a lounge suit.

In the days of Sir Thomas's father, when there had not only been family prayers in the hall but Sunday afternoon service in the chapel and no games on Sunday (the late Lady Vayne had been very pious), the Servants' Balls were much more full-blooded affairs and had included exhibitions of clog dancing by the keepers. But, coincident perhaps with the reign of Truelove, they had become more sedate and genteel. Now only the head keeper attended, and instead of clog dancing there was the military two-step, during which the gentlemen, though of course hatless, had to give their partners a military salute. There was also the Valeta, and of course the Lancers. From time to time the house party would visit the dining-room, where refreshments were laid out (needless to say there was an equally lavish supply of good things to eat and drink below stairs), and all too quickly the time fled, till it was nearly midnight. Then Truelove would reappear for the singing of 'Auld Lang Syne,' which was done in the usual way, everybody linked in a large circle, during which procedure Sir Thomas's face was a study in martyrdom. As the singing ended, the first strokes of midnight would sound from the clock on the front of the house. Then came a chorus of "Happy New Year," and "*Bonne Année*" from Pérez and Madame Pérez; and the house party would retire to bed, leaving a clear field for the others to dance till five in the morning. This they never failed to do; and the housemaids would leave the ballroom after 'God Save the King' only to take off their ball dresses and put on their print frocks without going to bed at all. They thought it well worth while, though all looked pale as ghosts throughout New Year's Day.

Phyllis was bent on a stolen visit to the scenes of the forthcoming revels. It rejoiced her heart to see those rooms, which for many months of the year remained shrouded and unused, come at last into their own. Once the gong had sounded she knew there was little danger of meeting anyone who was likely to challenge her right to be still up and about, punctuality at meals being one of the things about which Sir Thomas was really fussy; and everybody respected his wishes.

Down the back stairs she sped, through the door into the first floor corridor, turned right, then left, and down the short flight of stairs which brought her to the hall.

Some of the lights were already on and two card tables were set out in the central space under the chandelier. Two large Chippendale sofas faced each other at right angles to the fire. Behind one of them was the grand piano, and behind that the tall lacquer screen covered with fire birds and dragons.

She stood between two of the giant pillars and recollections of last Christmas crowded upon her as she surveyed the scene—boisterous fooling, small drolleries, trivial actions expressive of light-hearted joy, all contributing to form the dazzling pattern of delight which the word Christmas conveyed to her mind. Several brands of humour helped to compose this pattern. Piers's—rather concerned with the 'usual offices'; Mr. Blunt's more subtle and sophisticated; Uncle William's—rollicking, child-like and obvious.

Last New Year's Eve she had stood here, with Hilda and Alethea, the boys and Uncle Andrew, examining the cleared floor just before the ball, standing under the chandelier joking about the absence of mistletoe. Truelove would not, of course, allow such a vulgarism. Suddenly someone behind her, she did not know who, but probably Richard, had lifted her up till her face was on a level with Uncle Andrew's, who of course kissed her. Undoubtedly the peak of enjoyment was reached on New Year's Eve. Thereafter there would be the three glorious evenings of the theatricals, but they were overshadowed by the impending break up of the house party and the return to normal routine.

She wondered what games they would play to-night. Perhaps they would not play games and instead Cousin Amy would give them a little music. She played music of the lighter kind charmingly, Strauss and Lehar, bits out of Véronique and Offenbach's 'Barcarolle' which Lettice loved, but not much Beethoven or Brahms.

All music sounded well in the hall, even the most mediocre, but when on rare occasions beauty of composition was matched by its performance the sensitive listener might fancy a strange quickening of the atmosphere, as if the figures in the tapestries stirred with life, the very flowers in their vases trembled with yearning and delight. On the whole, however, the inmates of Vyne were not very sophisticated in their musical tastes, preferring Offenbach to Bach, Verdi to Beethoven or Brahms, and Strauss or Sullivan to any of these.

Yes, thought Phyllis, it all looked lovely; now she would have just one peep at her favourite room and then she must really be off to bed.

Leaving the hall by the opposite side from which she had entered, she mounted the corresponding short flight of stairs which led to the drawing-room.

Cautiously she opened the door in case by chance Grandmamma should already be installed there; but no, there was nobody in the room, which was lit only by firelight. It leapt over the bosses of the ceiling and threw inky shadows from the high reliefs of the plaster frieze, drew gleams of gold from the baskets of fruit on the heads of the caryatides flanking the chimney-piece and the Chippendale mirrors on the wall. It lit the polished

The room was lit by firelight only

shoulders of the Chinese goddesses, but the stained glass windows showed only as dim oblongs in the darkness of the bay.

As she crossed the room to the fireplace a shadowy reflection of herself crossed the room in the mirrors between the windows on the front of the house. She wanted to sit for just a little while in this room which she loved so well, this rich old treasure-house of a room, with its spicy aromatic smell, the leaping firelight and darting black shadows. She was a child who suffered from night fears. Stories of ghosts and witches so delightful in cheerful company returned to trouble her when alone in the dark. It was impossible ever to feel fear in the drawing-room—there could surely never be a room more conducive to peace of mind—but the Long Gallery, so enchanting a playground, could be a little frightening at night, and generally Phyllis avoided going there alone after dark. One night last summer holidays, however, resentful and unhappy from what she considered an unjust rebuke by her parents, she had run there, and flinging herself on one of the deep window seats, burst into tears of self-pity. The full moon was flooding into the gallery and the floor was barred with long rectangles of light cast from each uncurtained window. They lay in diminishing perspective down the whole great length of the room, completely changing its familiar aspect, and the effect, though beautiful, was weird and unearthly. But for once Phyllis's sense of woe was stronger than her fears of the supernatural. She sat in the full flood of the moonlight and wept with that complete abandonment to grief out of all proportion to the cause, of which only children are capable. Nobody loved her, her parents misjudged her, they expected too much, her most innocent words, devoid of any intention to offend, were taken the wrong way. She was misunderstood, lonely, desolate and oppressed.

But almost at once, breaking in upon her grief with a gentle but increasing pressure, she seemed to detect a sympathy in the surrounding atmosphere as if unseen presences thronging about her were offering their love and consolation. She thought there were many present, but felt neither surprise nor fear. Why else had she come,

In the full flood of the moonlight

to be alone and apart in this dark mysterious old room if not to seek and find comfort? After only a little while, grateful and happy again, she went to her room and to sleep.

Meantime, of course, she must not sit too long in the drawing-room. Withers, whose duty it was, would soon be coming to turn on the lights and see that everything was in order, and then Grandmamma after her little dinner in her room would come in on the arm of her maid to take up her place on the sofa by the fire.

Grandmamma too suffered from nervous fears, not of the supernatural but of flesh-and-blood burglars. She could hardly be left a moment alone on account of this. One morning last holidays Phyllis, forgetting that Grandmamma had been allotted the room usually given to Cousin Amy, had rapped loudly on the door and rattled the doorhandle. She was coming to fetch Cousin Amy for a walk. But the door was locked, and instead of the cheerful voice she expected, to her dismay, Grandmamma and her mother had replied, calling to whoever it might be to come round to the dressing-room next door where the maid slept and state his or her business. Instead of doing so, Phyllis took to her heels. Go round and explain her foolish mistake at length, not she, and later at luncheon she listened in guilty silence as her mother recounted the episode.

"Poor dear Mamma! She really is quite obsessed by this fear of burglars. Just now while I was sitting with her someone knocked on the door, but didn't come round to the dressing-room though we told them to. Then I noticed Mamma was feverishly keeping me in conversation till Wright should be back from her lunch, and at last she confessed she was afraid that the person who had knocked was a burglar. 'But the door's well locked, they can't get in,' she said." Sir Thomas remarked caustically that he didn't know burglars were in the habit of knocking loudly on bedroom doors before entering to do their burgling; and there, to Phyllis's great relief, the matter ended.

It was very still in the drawing-room. The clock ticked, the coals stirred in the grate, but no sound came from the nearby dining-room where by now they must be in the middle of dinner, but there were two closed doors and the intervening anteroom between. Sitting looking up at the arms of Elizabeth over the chimney-piece with the golden lion and the brown griffin (her mother had told her about the unicorn only coming in with the Stuarts), Phyllis thought: "How wonderful that in all the wide world there should be a 'me,' a person called Phyllis Vayne!" She could never get used to the wonder of personal identity. It was even more wonderful than having Vyne for a home. But supposing her father's prophecies were fulfilled. If a day should come when they would have to abandon Vyne? Oh, if that should happen how could she bear it? It would be like abandoning a helpless, loving fellow-creature—like leaving Lady to starve.

But these unwelcome thoughts and fears were only fleeting. Fear of the future, remote possibilities could not long trouble her, secure and unassailable in her glorious golden present.

The present was so full and vital it was impossible to imagine that it would not endure for ever. She jumped up, flinging her arms into the air for joy.

The fire leapt and crackled, the needlework-covered chairs drawn up round it waited for their occupants. There was such an air of happy expectancy about the old room that it stirred Phyllis's heart. Did it rejoice in being used, she wondered—just as it had been used by all those people, now long gone, her forbears, who had made it what it was?

"Oh," thought Phyllis, giving a last look round, "how I love you!" and fancied she caught a soundless response:

"Love me, love me, for I love you too!"

As she turned to go the old English clock on the table by the door struck the half-hour, then started to chime a Jacobite air.

Rapt with happiness, pleasure in the present beauty of the scene, anticipation of the joy which the morning would bring, the child waited till the tiny melody was over, then lifted her hand, half in farewell, half in unconscious benediction: "Lovely, beautiful room, goodnight."

Returning along the passage from the drawing-room, sure enough she encountered Withers, on his way there. He gave her a sardonic look in passing and pursed his lips, conveying wordlessly that she had no right to be there at that hour.

Withers was rather pleased with himself; but small wonder, for with the face and figure of Apollo, he was the idol of the women servants.

Louisa, who was waiting for Phyllis in her room, looked rather fierce and began at once to grumble.

"Miss Phyllis! You naughty girl, whatever have you been doing? Here have I been waiting about ever since Miss Lettice went down to dinner. Look at the time! Long after half past eight, and you ought to be in bed by quarter past. And what about my supper?"

Like Fräulein, Louisa was remarkable in that she spoke English just as well as her native tongue; but unlike Fräulein, though she was supposed to speak nothing else with Phyllis, not a word of French ever passed her lips.

"Oh, Louisa, you can't be cross to-night. I only went to have a look at the drawing-room; it looks so nice when it's ready for visitors"—a deliberate understatement. "Besides, if we hurry you won't be late for your supper."

"Come along, then, do." Louisa pounced on her and began to untie her sash.

"What a sight you must have looked with your sash tied like this!"

Quickly she divested Phyllis of her muslin frock and hustled her into her dressing-gown, then pushed her on to the dressing-stool and began to brush her hair.

Alas, it was not merely a question of brushing. Laid out on the dressing-table were layers of thin paper, more than a dozen of them, into which poor Phyllis's hair would have to be tightly screwed. Lucky Alethea! She could sleep all night in her loose curls and in the morning they only needed brushing and combing to look entrancing. It never occurred to anybody to leave Phyllis's hair in its natural state. Little girls must have curls, if not natural, then manufactured ones.

Overflowing with spirits and despite the coming ordeal, Phyllis broke into a catchy music-hall song: "Teasing, teasing, I was only teasing you."

Last year it had been: "I wouldn't leave my little wooden hut for you!" They had all sung it standing round the piano whilst Cousin Amy played the accompaniment. A 'glee' Cousin Amy had called it. They would be certain to sing more glees this Christmas.

Teasing, teasing! to find out if your love is true—
Don't be angree, I was only, only teasing you.

"Do be quiet and let me brush your hair," Louisa snapped. "How can I do it if you keep throwing your head about like that?"

Only slightly dashed, Phyllis stopped singing and began to prattle. Generally she read a book whilst the tedious hair-drill was going on, but to-night she wanted to talk about all the wonderful things now only so short a distance removed in time; to question Louisa about her dress for the ball and about the other maids' dresses, for she took a keen interest in this and sometimes proffered her advice. What a pity Truelove disapproved of dancing! He would make such a perfect master of ceremonies and would be certain to dance beautifully.

Truelove revolving slowly with the charmer in the décolleté dress would have been a sight worth seeing.

But nobody thought of questioning his decisions. Everyone, including Sir Thomas, but with the possible exception of Mrs. Campbell, was a little afraid of him.

It was impossible to imagine anything disturbing his serene calm and rather awful dignity; unthinkable that he should ever lose his temper. Nevertheless, if anything had displeased him the whole house knew it; equally, if the reverse had happened, everyone benefited, George not the least.

In genial condescension, smiling benignly on those beneath him, his mental as well as social inferiors, he might be said to find his true expression. Would Phyllis ever forget that day when, her parents being away, they had all sallied forth after lunch to play golf, six or eight of them driving off almost simultaneously from the first tee, Truelove in a long, elegant tweed overcoat and cap a little on one side. He was not playing himself but presiding over and directing the efforts of the others.

"Miss Phyllis, your ball's in the rushes; you'd better have another." And out he pulled a beautiful new 'Colonel.' "Yes, Miss Pont, you missed the globe, but you need not count that. Mr. Withers, I don't think you'll carry the rough with that cleek. No, Mr. Swan, I don't play myself." They were all striking out wildly when and how they pleased—it was a wonder nobody got hurt. In fact, poor Lady *was* a casualty, as Phyllis, taking a swipe at her

ball, actually got under and hit it fair and square, catching Lady, who was standing about thirty feet in front of the tee, broadside on.

"Do you think Papa will like his tie?" Phyllis, whose head was now half-surrounded by curl-papers, next asked Louisa.

"Of course he will. You've knitted it very well too," said Louisa, giving one more screw to a curler. Certainly thought Phyllis, her father did seem to like the presents one gave him, though he said less at the time than her mother. Once she had given him what she now knew to be a terrible little gilt rack like a toast-rack, intended for holding letters. It had a crimson glass blob on it, and her father had admired this in particular, saying it was like an eye. The little monstrosity still stood on his writing-table. It was odd, thought Phyllis, how quickly one's ideas of what was beautiful and desirable changed as one acquired a little more knowledge.

Much of this kind of education, often unconsciously given, she received from her mother.

Only the other day she and Mrs. Campbell had been waiting in one of the visitors' bedrooms for Lady Vayne to come and pass judgment on a number of eiderdown quilts sent down from London for her approval.

The housekeeper and the little girl had spent the time of waiting in admiring inspection of the quilts. What lovely colours! What beautiful glossy satin! They vied with each other in delighted approbation. It would be hard to decide, thought Phyllis—were one lucky enough to have the chance—whether to choose the scarlet satin piped with gold braid or the turquoise blue patterned with lilies and roses.

Then, suddenly entering with her quick, assured step, Lady Vayne completely changed the situation: "What appalling, vulgar things! What frightful colours! I couldn't possibly keep any of these! Mrs. Campbell, you must send them all back, at once."

Instantly, Phyllis perceived that her mother was right and she and Mrs. Campbell had been wrong. She saw the quilts with fresh eyes. They *were* vulgar and would have appeared so even in an hotel bedroom; how much more, then, in these dignified old rooms!

But poor Mrs. Campbell's discomfiture was complete. Though not actually chosen by herself, it was she who had instructed the London shop, telling them to be sure and send their very best. And now they would all have to go back.

Perhaps realising how things were, Lady Vayne tempered the disappointment with a graceful gesture. "Mrs. Campbell, you need a new eiderdown for your bedroom. Choose one now, any one you like."

Stepping forward and selecting the least flamboyant from among the gaudy pile, Mrs. Campbell said: "This one please, m'Lady." And the incident was closed.

Then, too, one learnt gradually not to use phrases one had used in the nursery—like the time when idly leafing through the *Graphic* she had remarked aloud: "The Duchess of D—— She's the grand dame of society, isn't she?" The words appearing below a photograph of a rather haughty-looking elderly lady in *Home Chat*, which Nana (since departed this life) always bought, had caught her eye. "Twice a duchess—the 'grande dame' of society," ran the caption in *Home Chat*. Now, seeing the photograph again in the *Graphic*, she remembered the phrase and repeated it, her own anglicised version giving it an added absurdity. She thought it sounded very grown-up. Only Lettice's slightly scornful smile and her father's amused expression told her she had said something odd.

Lettice was the person whose taste could always be relied upon. She invariably knew what people would like in the way of presents. The only trouble was the money difficulty. There was rather a lack of balance in the

[92]

Vyne household—Sir Thomas with his insistence on simplicity throwing his weight on one side of the scale, Lady Vayne, powerfully supported by Truelove, on the other.

The family never travelled between Vyne and London without a special saloon, two compartments of four seats, and the servants had reserved carriages. In London Sir Thomas rarely used the carriage, leaving it at his wife's disposal, but he hardly ever took a cab. On Sunday afternoons after a visit to the Zoo, where they spent much time trailing round the aviaries, he would often make Hilda and Phyllis walk a part of the way home before hailing a hansom. Pocket money was rather hard to come by, yet if cash were needed for an expedition to Hampton Court or the Tower of London, Fräulein had only to send down word by George the hallboy and back he would come with a little pile of change. No sum was specified; Truelove sent what he thought they should have, and it never erred on the side of parsimony!

They had a friend who owned an oyster bed on his property and sometimes, in return for the lavish hospitality of Vyne, sent a present of a barrel of oysters. Phyllis, who acquired an instant liking for them the very first time of tasting one, asked naïvely why they only had oysters when they had been sent as a present. Sir Thomas said one ought not to waste money on one's stomach; yet even Phyllis could see that Pérez's catering was not done on the cheap.

It irked her terribly that all her clothes except party frocks (and they were plain enough) should be made at home, and she had long decided what to do when she grew up and married. All her clothes would come from

Madame Hayward in Bond Street, where her mother only went for her best dresses, and she would buy oysters to eat whenever she fancied them. She would always give money in the street to anybody who begged from her, and send cheques to individuals in distress, not to charitable institutions where you never knew who got what. That the money for all this should always be forthcoming she took for granted, as also that other people's households were run on the same lines as at Vyne. Before lessons in the schoolroom had started seriously for her, she had been wont to spend the early part of the morning after her parents' breakfast in her mother's boudoir. Busy with her doll or a picture-book on the hearthrug, she was present at a succession of interviews, an invariable part of the day's routine.

The first was with Truelove, and lasted a few minutes. Then came a short pause whilst Lady Vayne started to deal with her correspondence, dashing her quill pen across the paper at the rate which always amazed her children. Then Pérez would enter in his speckless white and proffer a large open exercise book with a low bow. There would follow a slight discussion in French while Lady Vayne inspected the proposed menus for the day. Generally she would run her pencil through one or two items which she considered redundant, then return the book to the chef, who took it with another low bow and left the room.

After him came Mrs. Campbell, and lastly Archer, the head gardener.

Phyllis in after years retained a clear impression of her mother being at each interview in complete control of the situation. Yet was this really so? Certainly not in the first case, however much appearances might indicate it.

Truelove was unquestionably the 'Éminence Grise,' the power behind the throne, holding the reins of government; with the ear of the queen, the confidence and (albeit reluctant) admiration of the reigning monarch, and with both titular rulers dependent on him and knowing it. Considerably below him in stature, Pérez was certainly master of his particular department and in it carried on as he pleased.

The same to a lesser extent might be said of Mrs. Campbell, though the mere fact of her sex made Lady Vayne—perhaps unconsciously—rate her capabilities less highly than those of the other two.

The last of the morning visitors, Archer, ranked lowest in his mistress's esteem. Throughout the year his task was to fill the house, either at Vyne or in London, with flowers, ranging from almost every variety of stove plant, lilies, orchids and great frilly malmaisons to the small bunch of violets, their stalks wrapped in silver paper, which every day Phyllis carried into her mother's room and presented with her morning kiss. Out of doors, with soil and climate stubbornly uncooperative, he had to keep the herbaceous borders blazing with colour and full to overflowing (Lady Vayne did not like to see the earth) from mid July till October, provide a plentiful supply of bedding plants for the formal gardens and beds, keep the lawns and topiary work in perfect condition, and nurse and propagate the flowering trees and shrubs. In addition, he had to keep the huge household supplied with fruit and vegetables the whole year round. Though he had the assistance of an able foreman-gardener and about a dozen other underlings, it remained a difficult and exacting job, which on the whole he performed well.

In spite of this, however, he was subjected to constant interference as well as a good deal of criticism. Up and down the paths and terraces of Vyne he had to trudge beside his lightly tripping mistress, listening to her strictures and advice, though if called upon she could probably not have distinguished between a rose-sucker and a young healthy shoot.

In addition to this, a friend of the family who was a keen amateur gardener had been given *carte blanche* to come every summer to Vyne to lay down the law and generally interfere. If Sir Thomas or anybody, moved to pity for the luckless Archer, intervened on his behalf Lady Vayne would reply: "I must be allowed to wallop my own jackasses."

Even Mrs. Campbell seemed to despise and flout him. Once strolling in the garden with Hilda and Phyllis, they met Archer on his way to the house with a basket of hot-house fruit. Pausing for a minute or two of friendly chat, Mrs. Campbell drew attention to one of the cranes which had strayed from its paradisal surroundings, the wood and water garden known as Kill-Time. Whilst Archer turned to observe the crane she deftly abstracted two of the best peaches from his basket and presented them to the children as soon as he had gone on his way. Most decidedly poor Archer's lot was not a bed of roses.

Phyllis's head was now completely surrounded by curl-papers.

"There," said Louisa, and gave a final twist to each one in turn. "Now hurry up and get to bed, and don't forget your teeth. You must be asleep, you know, before Santa Claus comes."

"Don't say that—Papa hates it."

"Well, Father Christmas, then; but I'm sure I don't know why."

There were a few, though only a few, figures of speech to which Sir Thomas took violent exception. People who wrote, 'Thanking you in anticipation.' People who were rather consciously Irish in accent and idiom, and people who talked about 'Santa Claus' might ultimately win his approval, but they certainly started with the odds against them. Phyllis said the words 'Santa Claus' sounded extraordinarily ugly. "Yes," said her father, "but can't you see they're all wrong? Santa means a woman."

Yet he liked and felt at ease with people who thought and acted very differently from himself provided they were their own unaffected selves. Small absurdities and incongruities at which children laugh gave him innocent amusement also.

Lady Vayne possessed, together with a strong sense of the ridiculous, a rather dangerous gift of mimicry, in which her husband delighted.

A stout, middle-aged bachelor who lived in the village sometimes came up to lunch and play golf, accompanied by two Clumber spaniels which occasionally retrieved the balls that Phyllis with her newly acquired slice often sent into the rough.

Lady Vayne, having reproduced with the exact tone, voice and almost the look, one of his rather incongruous utterances, when another visit was pending: "You've got to make Brett say he's 'faddy,'" ordered her husband, sounding the 'a' in the North Country fashion.

But when the time came and the attempt seemed to fail, suddenly from behind the cover of his newspaper and quite inconsequently, "Are you faddy, Brett?" asked Sir Thomas, and then gave a smothered guffaw, for which he was afterwards scolded.

Being quite devoid of malice, he was also incapable of flattery or even diplomatic evasion. He said outright what other people only thought, and sometimes what they did not think if they were self-deceivers.

Once when they were discussing a new acquaintance, Sir Thomas asked if he were married.

Lady Vayne said she did not know but had seen him at the play one night with a large fat woman.

"Then that settles it," said Sir Thomas. "Of course he's married. Nobody takes a large fat woman to the play for pleasure."

Yet speeches such as this belied an innate chivalry, so shy of expression that it could only show itself in the least obvious ways: in his objection to calling any of the women servants by their surnames unless with the prefix 'Mrs.', in his manner when speaking to them, which he rarely did, just as he would to his wife's women friends.

He would praise their skill and industry and never complain about them, though he sometimes did of the men; on the contrary, if Lady Vayne were doing so, he always took up their defence even if he knew nothing about them. The supply of house, kitchen and laundry maids was still plentiful. He knew they would find it harder to get another good place than Mrs. Campbell would to find substitutes. This tenderness towards women of the humbler kind extended also to females of the bird and animal world—in his feeling for Lady compared with Mike and for hen pheasants at a shoot.

"Listen to that unfortunate bird," he said once when the mate of one of the cranes had died and the plaintive calls of the bereaved one were echoing through Kill-Time. No one had noticed it till then, but it was clear that the grief of the poor widow bird calling and calling for her vanished mate wrung his heart.

Sir Thomas was perfectly consistent. All display was vulgar—the display of one's own goodness of heart most vulgar of all. So only the recipients knew of his many acts of charity. His light did not shine before men that they might see his good works. He did good by stealth and hid his light under a bushel.

After Louisa had left her, Phyllis sat for a while in the old plush-covered armchair by the fire thinking her Christmas thoughts.

Her red-curtained bed waited invitingly with the sheet turned down. She had placed it along the wall so that the curtains spread over head and foot gave it a tent-like appearance. Her stocking hung at the bed-foot, but it was now little more than a symbol, a traditional rite to be observed, and it was never filled with anything more exciting than nuts, almonds and raisins, sweets and tangerines. Last year though wide awake she had lain quietly feigning sleep whilst Father Christmas in the guise of Mrs. Campbell entered rather noisily, breathing rather heavily and groping about in the dark, spilling several nuts in the process, filled her stocking and retired again.

To the right of the door stood the little glass-fronted cabinet made for her in the Vyne workshop to hold her collection of Goss china. On the top of the Victorian wardrobe sat the two early-Victorian dolls, a boy and a girl with china faces, dressed in heavy, dark-coloured clothes. The Jacobean chest-of-drawers was a twin to the one in the Oak Room; several handles had been off it for a long time; and on the wall behind her, tilted forward at an angle, hung a long, very narrow cheval glass; there was one exactly like it in her mother's bedroom.

Phyllis loved her room, as indeed she did every room at Vyne. She could have identified any one of them if led into it blindfold by its individual smell. The 'Room' smelt of beer and coco-nut matting, the still-room of hot cakes and scones, the schoolroom was a blend of Mike, Lady, ink and Fräulein's cough drops. Her father's study smelt of tobacco, Harris tweed and Russian leather; her mother's boudoir of violets and sealing-wax. The drawing-room had the most distinctive smell of all and the hardest to define—it seemed to be composed of spices, pot-pourri, beeswax and the past. The combined essence of all these individual scents which made the peculiar fragrance belonging to Vyne was one of the first things one noticed on returning there from London, and most of all at Easter.

They would drive up through the park from the station, mounting gradually all the time, and Sir Thomas would remark that the grass had not yet started to grow. But Phyllis could discern the look and smell of Easter in the keen northern air, would notice the green spikes of the daffodils with only here and there a narrow golden bud— for spring came late to Vyne. They would turn in at the forecourt gates, the dogs leaping up to welcome them as they got out. John's face above his yellow striped waist-coat would be ruddy and smiling, and Mrs. Campbell would be there too.

But after she had greeted them, Phyllis would rush, not out to the garden, but up the back stairs, closely followed by Lady, to her dear waiting bedroom, and the sweet fresh smell of it after London was not the least of her joys. So it must always have been—its sons and daughters yearning for it when they were away. "Dear Vyne—Sweet Vyne," they wrote in that crabbed writing Lady Vayne was to risk her eyesight in deciphering. "My dearest Deare," wrote Richard Vayne, the Member of Parliament, from Charles II's London to his wife at Vyne, "would that I were at home with thee and the deare brats." And just so to-day, the Vaynes when in London yearned for their northern home.

Fräulein was playing Wagner's 'Fire Music' in the adjoining schoolroom. Phyllis liked to hear it after she had gone to bed; the sound of the piano was friendly and comforting if, as did not happen often now, her night-fears were upon her.

Slowly and at leisure, she began her bedtime toilet. She liked the mottled blue and white of her jug and basin, simulating marble, but Lettice had a prettier set with a pattern of acorns round the edges. The brown hot-water can always smelt of hot enamel and flakes of it sometimes came off in the water.

She wondered whether Alethea was asleep by now or lying awake joyfully anticipating the morrow. It must be wonderful to be Alethea, but if by some magic they could exchange personalities she knew that she would never do so.

To-morrow she would be moving in a maze of enchantment through the drama dance of Christmas, that drama in which the setting played so great a part. Waking in the twilight of the winter's morning, waiting for the singing in the courtyard, the herald of the day's delights. Breakfast and the exchange of small gifts. The visit to her parents' rooms together with her brothers and sisters to give them their joint offerings. Then the drive down through the white park to the old church—the familiar Christmas service—"And it came to pass in those days, that there went out a decree from Caesar Augustus, that all the world should be taxed." A very short sermon from Mr. Hunt and the lovely Christmas hymns. Home again for luncheon, with the table stretching almost the whole length of the big room. The boar's head on the sideboard. The joking and fooling in the library. Then out-of-doors for a little exercise, snow-balling perhaps if there was enough snow, then in again to change for tea in the dining-room with lovely iced cakes and crackers. And then the joyous chattering throng climbing the stairs to the Long Gallery.

And there would stand the great shimmering blazing tree, the only light in the room except the fire, and beside it the bran tub, so full that some of the packages were not quite submerged, and beyond the radius of the tree's light the great long room stretching away into the shadows.

They would begin by drawing out the presents one at a time. "Phyllis, with love from Papa and Mamma." "Alethea, with love from Uncle Tom and Aunt Evy." But very soon the tempo would quicken, till they were all pulling them out together. It would seem to go on for ages. And then there was the almost equal delight of examining one's own and other people's presents and playing with them, and then the little pause before it was time to get ready for dinner. There seemed no end to the delights, and all the time and independent of all this that strange, indescribable feeling in the air which

The great shimmering tree

only came at Christmas. "Oh, Heaven, Heaven!" thought Phyllis, getting ready for bed.

One day (and this was hard to believe) she would be an old woman and would have to die. One hoped at death to go to one's true home. She was past the stage when one verse in the hymn 'There's a Friend for Little Children' evoked visions of gold crowns kept in the nursery cupboard ("Nana, can I wear my crown this morning?"). But her childish mind could only take in purely anthropomorphic images. Life in heaven must

be life at Vyne with all the highspots of delight eternally
repeated and prolonged, with all the people she knew
and loved around her, and God the Son sometimes
coming over the moors to visit them walking on the
water.

Phyllis resolved to be up and waiting for the carol
singers when they came in the morning. Were they not
the herald angels of whom they would afterwards be
singing in church, the overture to the Christmas drama,
the bringers of the glad tidings of great joy? There was
not long to wait now before the drama would begin—
the curtain was trembling to its rise. The twilight of the
early winter morning, the piercing sweetness of the
voices rising in the still air, the tune and the words she
loved so well, "Christians, awake, salute the happy
morn!"

Then heaven would open.

Epilogue

1946

ONE MISTY DAY OF LATE SUMMER A SMALL MOTOR CAR CON-
taining two middle-aged women and a young man drew
up outside one of the entrances to Vyne Park.

"I'll ask the lodge-keeper if we can go through," said
the woman who was driving. "You stay here, Phyllis,
it'll be easier for me than for you."

She got out and went and spoke to somebody at the
open window of the grey stone lodge, then very soon
came back and said it was going to be all right.

"We ought, of course, to have gone to the main
entrance and up the front drive, but when I told her who
we were she said she'd give me the key of the second gate.
But she says we must be careful in case we meet another
car."

The lodge-keeper handed them the key as they passed
through, and Phyllis looked hard at the woman, but she
did not know her face.

She had been visiting her old friend and neighbour of
childhood for the first time since the war. Celia was one
of the few survivors still clinging on precariously, using
every possible device, every lawful expedient to retain
their ancient heritage, crippled with taxes, harassed by
controls, uncertain how long they could go on or
whether after all their children would be able or at liberty

to live in their old homes. Nevertheless, and however precarious her hold, Celia was still here, but the Vaynes were gone. Vyne now belonged to the nation.

They went on slowly up the stony, broken drive; the undergrowth had encroached so much it would have been very awkward if they had met anything. This was Wishing Well Wood. There should have been pheasants rising cumbersomely with a clatter of wings, almost ready for the shoot in a few weeks' time, rabbits too bounding away up the steep hillside, but as they went they saw no sign of life. There was the turning to the quarry, and a little further on should be the clearing with the wishing well. Phyllis looked carefully, but she could not see it; the rhododendrons and bracken must have grown up round the little stone basin and hidden it from view, and the stream after the long dry summer was only a thin trickle.

They came to the second gate, and Robert, Celia's son, got out and unlocked it. They passed out of the wood into the wild, open country with hills on either side, but the outcrop of rock near the entrance to the wood, the tawny-yellow stone, almost rose-coloured in places, from which the garden front of the house had been built seemed to have vanished also. There were no sheep or deer now to keep the grass close cropped; how tussocky and rough it had become, and surely there were far more rushes! Celia stopped the car just before the steep dip in the road with the two ancient lime trees on either side and they got out and started to walk down the drive. It was very still and the mist hid the more distant hills. Celia complained of the flies bothering her. Then they rounded the bend, and there was the house confronting them across the valley.

It was the view painted on the drop curtain—the great house standing upon its high-buttressed walls, the bright parterre of the Italian garden outspread beneath; the white plume of the fountain in the centre for ever rising and falling, and the sound of it very clear and distinct carried across the intervening valley on the still, windless air.

All this was just as in the old days, and yet there was something strange about the appearance of the house, a subtle difference—but what it was Phyllis could not at once discern. Then as they drew nearer she saw what it was.

The windows were no longer bright and gleaming, but shuttered and opaque; no longer looking out across the valley, they were blind eyes or eyes closed in sleep.

They went on to the foot of the hill and saw that on the flat expanse of ground below the garden the turf had been removed to make a huge car park for the visitors.

They turned aside through the gate into the meadow, where if they mounted to its top they could see the house again on the garden side at the end of the lime avenue. From there it should not look very different from former times. There were pieces of paper in the rank grass in front of the gate. Sometimes in the old days there had been paper lying about after a Bank Holiday when a lot of trippers had come, but never so much as now. How they had resented those trippers, thought Phyllis, and now she was revisiting her old home as a tripper herself. Not for the first time, she felt glad that her parents were no longer alive to see the changes time and a second world war had wrought.

For Sir Thomas the surrender of Vyne to Richard

soon after the first war had been no matter for regret; rather the contrary. He could still visit the old place where his son and daughter-in-law now reigned without any feeling of dispossession but only of relief at the lifting of a heavy burden of responsibility. But for Lady Vayne the sacrifice had been great. She had done it in order to save Vyne, for who at that time could foresee a yet more devastating war, one that would completely shatter all remnants of the old order. That her sacrifice should after all have been in vain would have been more than she could bear.

They went on up the steep, stony track which led to the wood at the end of the lime avenue; behind the wood were the moors. Here, too, the grass of the meadow which used to be fine pasture was rough and tussocky and great drifts of thistles spread all over it, their down without a breath of wind to stir it, hanging motionless on the stalks.

Celia was disturbed by the sight of the thistles. "I must speak to Charlie Withinshaw about it," she said. "He's more or less in command here, and they shouldn't be allowed to seed themselves over all the surrounding land."

Celia, in between her many activities, agricultural, political and social, had converted part of her ancient manor house into a very labour-saving flat for her own use, and as she still had two resident servants, English and properly trained, it was very pleasant staying with her. The rest of the house she and Robert were now proposing to throw open to the public at stated times as an additional source of income. Twice a week through much of the year tours, sometimes conducted by themselves, would go through the mediæval banqueting hall and Minstrels' Gallery, to view the organ on which Handel had composed a famous work and the manuscript in the master's own hand.

"We ought to charge two and six a head," said Robert, "and double for children." He spoke half in earnest.

They reached the wood and climbed the stile and then were able, as Phyllis had wished, to look back down the long lime avenue to the Palladian garden front of the house. The mist had lifted a trifle, and just over the pediment rose the bare, conical hill and on its summit, crowning it, the famous landmark for miles around, the tall old square tower, the Cage.

They stood in silence for a little while looking at the long façade, tawny-yellow in this light and too far off now to see whether the windows were shuttered or not. Probably they were, but the lawns were as brilliant a green as of old.

"Oh, I forgot to tell you," said Celia, "they're using the chapel again. They have afternoon services for the people who come to see the place. Charlie Withinshaw says there's quite a large attendance. They've done it up and it really looks lovely."

Here was a strange reversal of fortune. In the last glorious days of sunset (though they had not known it was the sunset) the chapel had been disused and neglected, a mere storehouse for surplus furniture. Now the glory of the house had departed, its motive for existence gone, but the chapel still unscathed, restored and beautified, was fulfilling the purpose for which it had been designed. This tiny grain of comfort seemed symbolical of an immense truth. After a few minutes they turned to go back the way they had come, but Phyllis wanted to go just a little further round the hillside till they could see the open moors at the back, and this they did. There was the familiar sweep of the hills, but no red deer were to be seen.

They walked slowly back down the hill through the gate at the bottom and up the hill again on the other side. Phyllis turned and looked back once more at the familiar view of the house, that view on the drop-curtain which so many artists and she herself had often sketched. Then they passed the two old lime trees and the house was hidden from view. In silence they drove back through Wishing Well Wood until they came to the lodge gate. An elderly man with a weather-beaten face and white hair came to open it for them, and he took the key from Celia.

"Thank you for letting us through," she said. "You know why we wanted to come, don't you?"

"Yes, madam, my wife told me. I used to work for Sir Thomas in the old days."

Phyllis looked at the rugged face, but for the life of her she could not place it.

"I remember Miss Hilda coming to my house for milk when they'd been out on the moors," he said, "she and another young lady who was staying."

"Do you remember me?" asked Phyllis.

"Yes, madam, I do."

He must have come during the first war, thought Phyllis, when they were all busy with hospital and Red Cross work and there were no flower shows or school treats or Christmas trees and no beef distribution on Christmas Eve (the war had finally put a stop to all that), otherwise she must have known him.

"It's nice to think some of the old people still live here," she said. "They seem to keep up the gardens well."

"Yes, madam, but it's not like the old days; they don't keep up the park like it used to be. No, it's not a bit like the old days."

Phyllis put her hand through the open window of the car and grasped his hand and shook it. She wanted to ask him if there were any more of the old people still living here, but she could not trust herself to say so much. "Goodbye," she said instead. And it was all she could say.

The other two began talking as they drove on, to give her time to recover, and very soon she did so, but still remained silent, busy with her thoughts.

Strange, dreamlike and unreal the Vyne she had just left had looked: far less real than the one which dwelt in her memory. Was it only the bleakness of the present which made those far-off scenes of childhood appear so joyous, tender and limned with gold? There had been times enough, if she had cared to delve deep into her memory, when even at Vyne she had been bored, discontented and unhappy, resentful of any injustice, chafing under control and critical of her elders and what she considered their failure to take full advantage of favoured circumstance. But for all that those past griefs now meant to her, they might never have been felt.

What, she wondered, had most contributed to the magic of those times, to the Christmas parties especially? The qualities of the people who composed them? Without the people, two or three in particular, there could have been no planning and carrying out of delightful pastimes, no fun and laughter, no delicious fooling. But place those same people in a different environment, and would the enchantment still have held?

Others might think differently, but for her the chief player in those dramas of delight had always been the house. In its fairyland setting, the palace on the edge of the lonely moors, it was the background which enhanced every action of the players—and just as in childhood, so now, as an ageing woman, the place had always seemed to her to be alive, teeming with the spirit poured into it by those who had created it, loved it, lived and died in it. But now it was dead, just as they were dead; it had died when it ceased to be a home.

But just as she believed that somewhere outside the track of time, where past and future merged into an Eternal Present, there was another world, the world of Ultimate Reality, so too she must hope that somewhere in that other world there was a place for Vyne where its spirit still lived together with its creators.

To-morrow she would be returning to London, the post-war London of bus and fish and cigarette queues; of dingy, littered pavements and shabby, paintless houses, of hatless men in pullovers and women with handkerchiefs round their heads and stockingless legs. Some people, and Henry her husband was one, could never grow reconciled to the complete destruction of the civilisation they had known. Nor did they find solace as she did in memories of the past, nor satisfaction in past achievements.

"When once you get a nation harping on its past glory, you may be sure that nation's on the down grade,"

Henry would say. "We never boasted of our great-
ness when we really were great—we took it all for
granted."

Nevertheless, she knew that they were fortunate who
had memories of a gentler world—a world before total
wars and atom bombs and horror camps and miserable
starving slaves.

Beautiful, gentle old world. Beautiful, sweet and gentle,
loved and loving old home.

But after all, its passing was only in the nature of all
earthly things; whether it was a world civilisation or a
human being, or a house. One aged and grew old and
one after another the things one valued—physical attrac-
tions, mental alertness, bodily vigour, friends, relatives,
dearest companions—the things of the body, the things
of the mind, the things of the heart—all were taken from
one, till at last one had to go as one had come, naked and
alone.

Very vividly a memory took shape in her mind. She
stood again with her brothers and sisters in the parish
church of Vyne at the conclusion of the service. Her
father was in his accustomed place in the chancel; at the
altar, tall, majestic like a piece of Graeco-Roman sculp-
ture, the white-robed figure of Canon Waldegrave.

The bearded sidesman with the squeaky boots was
going round with the velvet bag into which they would
drop their coins. Just in front of them were the ranks of
the surpliced choir—the little boys with Jim Bowden's
eldest son amongst them, and behind them the men led
by Mr. Swan, the schoolmaster, and behind them again
the young women, with Miss Bennet of the post office—
singing in their North Country accents, but very truly

and sweetly, the anthem they nearly always sang whilst
the collection was being made:

> "*Lay up for yourselves treasures in Heaven,*
> *where neither moth nor rust doth corrupt,*
> *and where thieves do not break through*
> *nor steal.*"

Peace be to this house.

Luke 10. 5